CW00348667

1 MONTH OF
FREE
READING

at
www.ForgottenBooks.com

By purchasing this book you are eligible for one month membership to ForgottenBooks.com, giving you unlimited access to our entire collection of over 1,000,000 titles via our web site and mobile apps.

To claim your free month visit:
www.forgottenbooks.com/free742700

ISBN 978-0-484-34469-2
PIBN 10742700

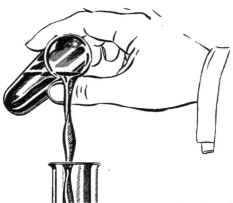

CHEMISTRY AND YOUR INVESTMENTS

Now harnessed to the war, chemistry and the science of electronics will work later to enrich our way of living. They promise far-reaching economic consequences after the war.

For these reasons it is essential that the owner of investments keep informed on new developments and their probable effect on the securities he holds.

Yet how many individuals have the facilities or the time to devote to such study? Have you?

Through its Personal Agency Service, the Rhode Island Hospital Trust Company can provide the constant analytical study of these and other factors which affect the value of securities and their earning power. Let us tell you, in detail, how this service can be employed to relieve you of the burden of managing your investments.

Cost Deductible on Income Tax

The costs of managing securities upon which taxable income is produced or sought are allowable deductions in determining net taxable income. In the light of this, the expense of our Agency Service is decidedly moderate.

Rhode Island Hospital Trust Company

Pawtucket—Providence—Woonsocket

ed monthly, January, August and September excepted, by the BROWN ALUMNI MONTHLY, Inc., at Brown University, nce, R. I. Entered at the Post Office, at Providence, R. I., as second class matter, under the law of March 3, 1879

BROWN
ALUMNI MONTHLY

PROVIDENCE, RHODE ISLAND
SUMMER, 1944
VOL. XLV   NUMBER 2

▶ ▶ Under the Heading of Commencement

▶ ▶, WE DID NOT SING Professor Everett's hymn "Commencement" this year in June. We did not remark that "from every State the sons of Brown who bear her torch aflame, return today to this dear shrine, the gift of youth to claim." As Charles E. Hughes, Jr., '09, the presiding officer at the Alumni Meeting in Sayles Hall, pointed out, the statement was hardly accurate nor the sentiment appropriate: the hymn had gone into reverse. Never have Brown men been so scattered over the face of the earth.

But it was a memorable Commencement for all that, even because of that. It was more than a run-through for tradition's sake. It had body—the alumni who came back "to pledge new love and zeal" made up no overwhelming crowd, far from that. But it had substance of thought, reminiscence, and utterance, too. And spirit. The spirit was deep, on the solemn side, humble, and very honest—like the Chaplain's prayer for the men overseas and over here in preparation. Sentimentalist or no, you were moved by this 176th annual Commencement for Brown University.

▶ THE RANKS of alumni and graduates were cut sharply, but there was the procession to the Meeting House, between showers. There were two Senior orations, one of which was reprinted in the New York Times magazine for July 16. In them, too, the war was reflected, for Carlton H. Gregory '44 spoke to the text written by an RCAF flyer, now dead: "We have cleared the site and laid the foundation. You build." And Nathaniel Davis '45, of a famous Brown family, also stirringly proclaimed the "Ideals We Fight For,"—one of them "to fashion a law under which nations can be free."

There were degrees for graduates, many of them in absentia, men in classes from 1942 to 1945. There were certificates to two other groups: 1. students leaving to continue their studies in medical school, USNR Midshipman's School, or Supply Corps school. 2. civilian students withdrawn from College to enter the armed services of their country and honored with this token of "academic achievement and patriotic devotion." There were in all degrees for 55 Brown Seniors and 51 Pembroke Seniors, for one Ph.D. candidate, and 11 other graduate students.

▶ FIVE THOUSAND Brown men, in the armed services, were too busy for reunions this year, but those at home who were near at hand carried out this gracious act of friendship in simple fashion that suited the time and the opportunity. There were not a half-dozen large reunions among the 25 reported, but even where they were only "token" affairs they were worth the holding. Major interest centred in the Classes of 1879—65 years out, the 60-year Class of 1884, 1894, 1899, 1919, and 1924, although the following should also be included in any reunion roll call for June, 1944: 1890, 1891, 1893, 1900, 1902, 1903, 1904, 1905, 1906, 1907, 1908, 1909, 1910, 1913, 1914, 1916, 1923, 1934, 1939. Details are given on pages 31-33.

An innovation which proved welcome was the opening of two guest houses for alumni—Horace Mann dormitory and Warren House. Both were well employed by out of town men attracted by the various reunions, all in or near Providence this year.

THE COVER PHOTO: Thayer Street is the scene, and members of the ROTC company of Brown's Navy V-12 unit are the personnel.

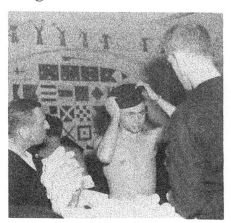

NEW SEMESTER, NEW SEAMAN: July 1 saw the campus starting on its third summer semester of the war. Replacements arrived for the Naval Unit, as well as 100 new civilian Freshmen.

Except for the special review of the Brown Naval unit Saturday morning on the Middle Campus, the Baccalaureate service on Sunday afternoon, and the President's reception which followed on the lawn before Faunce House, the principal parts of Commencement were consolidated in the morning of June 19. There was room for the alumni in the Church this year, and after the graduating exercises they climbed the Hill again for the Sayles Hall meeting held before lunch.

The Alumni Meeting, only a short business session a year ago, proved a very rewarding session. It began with the National Anthem, a robust singing. Henry C. Hart '01, President of the Associated Alumni, announced the alumni election results and introduced Mr. Hughes. The Vice-President announced gifts to Brown of more than $400,000. The Governor of the State brought a graceful greeting to the alumni and to Arthur Hays Sulzberger, one of the speakers. Mr. McGrath's good-humored reference to the autumn election brought a friendly laugh. Then we sang Henry R. Palmer's "Mother Dear, Brunonia," with C. LeRoy Grinnell '08 playing the organ in the loft which was familiar to him as an undergraduate. And behind the platform, hanging over the east window, was a new service flag for the University. The gold star represented 63, the blue star stood for 5041.

▶ WHAT DOES Brown University intend to do for the service man when he returns? President Wriston spoke to that point. The question could be answered briefly, he said: Don't exploit the returned veterans; educate them.

They were not to be used as educational guinea pigs, employed principally as a promotional device for a college, any more than they should be pandered to politically or exploited financially. Some of them were already back, and we were already helping them. We had discovered—as we knew we would—that they have been citizen soldiers. "Their citizenship is the foundation of their soldiery. Their citizenship, not their soldiery, is the permanent aspect of their lives. . . . When their part of the war is over, most of them hope their soldiering will be over, too."

The boys and 40 of our Faculty went away to war without bombast or parade. "They will return in the same manner. Each will come back as an individual." Returned soldiers will be taught, in part, by returned soldiers, too. These veterans teaching veterans will understand them, for they have shared experiences. We will have equipment for testing and counseling that will be of great assistance, "for Brown has never thought in terms of mass education" . . . rather, in individuation. ("It is well to remember that this

Tall Tale from Burma ◀

—photo of Ian Forman, courtesy of Mount Hermon School Alumni News.

High Enough for the Ghurkas

▶ ▶ IAN FORMAN '46' who has been in the thick of the fighting in Burma as a member of the A.F.S. ambulance corps, tells this one to fortify the fame of the Ghurkas and suggest their disciplined courage:

Some Ghurkas who were going to become paratroopers were told by their British sergeant that the first day they would all go up in a plane and jump 1000 feet. First the captain would jump, then the sergeant, and the rest would all follow in their turn. The little mountaineers went into a huddle, a great deal of chattering ensued, but they finally agreed that everything was all right. The second day they would all go up again, this time to jump from 2000 feet. Again the huddle, with more chattering on a higher pitch, but they agreed again to follow their officers. The sergeant continued: On the third day they would climb to 3000 feet before jumping.

There was great confusion following this announcement, and even after a great deal of discussion the Ghurkas could not reach a decision. At last one of their number stepped forward and told the sergeant that they were sorry—they could not jump from 3000 feet, but they were sorry—they could not jump from 3000 feet. The sergeant, quite taken aback, made the inevitable reply: "But the captain will jump from 3000 feet, and I shall jump from 3000 feet . . ."

"Yes, sahib, but you and the captain have parachutes." ◀ ◀

University has the longest record of educational testing and measurement of any institution in the country. . . . We have used them as a basis for guidance, but have not tolerated their abuse as a substitute for informed judgment.")

There will be opportunity for refresher courses, for the trained whose "technical experience and specialized skills have been short-circuited by their war service." In a new Department of Medical Sciences, advanced training can be given to those unable to return to medical schools but who wish to mature in their specialties. Similar opportunity, President Wriston hoped, would be available for other professions so that there would be facilities open to persons who "may come for credit, for academic recognition, for intensive review, for knowledge of new developments, or for more solid professional advancement." Situated as Brown is, we have an opportunity and a responsibility. "We shall not let precedent or custom offer barriers to service."

▶ "OUR GREATEST SERVICE," the President continued, "will be in the field of liberal education. Upon that rock this institution was founded; it remains upon the same foundation. . . . After their military life is over, the men will find themselves faced with the complexities of civilian life. They will no longer have to take orders, no longer be faced with a chain of responsibility which can be passed either upwards or downwards. . . . They will be in the paradoxical position of having vindicated the democratic thesis without having experienced it. . . .

"Comprehension is the function of the liberal arts, for they deal with man in all his relationships, at all times, and in all places. They grapple with fundamental human problems if they are honest and competent. The returning soldier will not want us to pretend to teach the liberal arts and then prostitute them to contemporaneity or distort them by emphasis primarily on training. Nor will the soldier want a liberal arts program to seek escape from the modern world. We do not need to choose between the new and the old; we can, and must, have both. . . .

"This is the great objective. It must come before all else in our program. The mastery of that task requires teachers with emotional balance, cultural awareness, intellectual alertness; they must have perspective, a profound respect for the ways of others both in time and space. The faculty must have courage to make changes but an equal readiness to cleave fast to that which is good. It is no extemporized ideal, no jerry-built program. To those ends this faculty has long been working; to those ends they must rededicate themselves in the future." (The complete text of Dr. Wriston's address is available on request at the News Bureau at Brown.)

▶ MR. SULZBERGER, the first speaker, made a deep impression on his audience at the Alumni Meeting. He offered three formulae for a lasting peace, for "more than an interim between wars": Universal military training; more interest by the press and the schools in the ends for which we fight; and more attention to our teachers. "I would not limit any freedom of study," he said, "but I think we are warranted in teaching our own democratic faith and history before we turn to the isms with which they are now at war."

The pre-war period was one of debunking—to become a cynic was thought to be growing up. Men abandoned their ideals and forgot the fault lay in the men. The new generation, he said, the soldiers are the heirs to our disillusionment, but both generations must jointly retain their basic faith in the American heritage of fair play and decency, pity and understanding, the Ten Commandments, Magna Carta, our Bill of Rights. We must "determine how best to avoid a renewal of the distrust between generations." He proposed to concentrate "on developing the co-operation we now have rather than on creating the machinery for co-operation."

Brown's Highest Compliment

▶ ONLY five times before had the Susan Colver Rosenberger Medal been conferred. The award, "for specially notable beneficial achievement," is within the power of the Brown Faculty to make, and it has come to be regarded as the highest compliment which the University can bestow. Henry D. Sharpe, Chancellor of the University since 1932, received it this June, during the graduation exercises. The citation was thus addressed:

"Today you are completing 50 years as an Alumnus of the University, four decades as a Trustee, and 12 years as its Chancellor. In these relationships you have consistently exhibited the temper and qualities of a scholar, the impulses and habits of a philanthropist. With unflagging zeal for the strengthening of this institution, you have been a staunch defender of academic freedom, the most sensitive manifestation of a really free society.

"Therefore the Faculty of Brown University confers upon you its most distinguished award for specially notable and beneficial achievement, and I have the honor, on its behalf, to present to you the Susan Colver Rosenberger Medal."

Previous recipients of the award were the late Dr. Charles V. Chapin '76' for his pioneer service in public health work; Chief Justice Fred T. Field '00' of the Massachusetts Supreme Court; John D. Rockefeller, Jr., '97; Charles Evans Hughes '81' retired Chief Justice of the United States Supreme Court, and Mary Emma Woolley of Mount Holyoke College, a member of the class of '94 at Pembroke.

Mr. Sharpe is President and Treasurer of the Brown and Sharpe Manufacturing Co. of Providence, whose affairs he has directed for 45 years. He holds offices and directorships in many other Rhode Island enterprises, civic and commercial both. He was the leading spirit at the time the Providence-Cranston Community Fund was set up and is permanent chairman of its board of directors. He has twice been President of the New England Council. To Brown University his services and benefactions have been manifold. ◀

Honorary Degree Citations

▶ THREE honorary degrees were conferred at the exercises in the Meeting House this June, to the Treasurer of the University, Harold C. Field '94; to Dr. Moses L. Crossley '09' Director of Research for the American Cyanamid Co.; and to Arthur Hays Sulzberger, publisher and president of the New York Times. The citations which accompanied them were as follows:

HAROLD CRINS FIELD, Master of Arts. For ten years you have made a gift of your full-time service as the Treasurer of the University. The discharge of those responsible duties has been a daily and tangible manifestation of the love you bear the college from which you graduated half a century ago. With industry and persistence, with humor and shrewdness, with thoughtfulness and wisdom, you have conserved and increased the material resources vital to its educational program. In honoring you we seek to express our deep sense of obligation and, even more, our warm affection.

· MOSES LEVEROCK CROSSLEY, Doctor of Science. In the universal drama of the modern world nothing exhibits the international character of the scientific spirit more fully than the development of the sulfa drugs. Your significant

contribution to that thrilling accomplishment is merely one example of the wealth of your imagination, the discipline of your skill, the eagerness of your search for the bases of healthier living. For originality and leadership, we are happy to do you honor, and to the three degrees in course earned upon this campus, we now add a fourth, as well and truly earned in the wider school of experience.

ARTHUR HAYS SULZBERGER, Doctor of Letters. Capital and labor; government and private enterprise; local and state, national and international impacts; objective impartiality and considered opinion; intensely human and infinitely mechanical; the modern metropolitan newspaper epitomizes in its own organization and reflects in its columns the marvelous diversity, the vast complexity, every tension, and every paradox of the modern world. The administration of such a trust in the spirit of statesmanship, with a mind singled to the public interest, and with devotion to the welfare of humanity, deserves acclaim. ◀

Ten Houses Deeded to Brown

▶ TEN of the Brown fraternities had deeded their chapter houses to the University at Commencement time when the Corporation unanimously adopted a resolution approving policy and procedure in its proposal to the fraternities. At the end of the meeting the following statement was issued by Claude R. Branch '07, member of the Board of Fellows designated to speak for the Corporation:

"An extended discussion of the problem of housing undergraduates, and particularly of the fraternity house matter, took place this afternoon at a meeting of the Corporation of Brown University. The meeting was largely attended, 37 members out of a total membership of 49 being present. A number of questions were asked and approval of the project, formally launched by a vote of the corporation at its meeting last October, was expressed by all who spoke.

"Members of the advisory and executive committee of 13, which had given particular attention to this matter, pointed out that the request for gifts of the chapter houses was but part of a larger plan for solving the housing problem in a manner best calculated to insure the future of the fraternity system. A full report was made of what the committee had done, and the corporation unanimously passed a vote approving of the steps which had been taken and directed the committee to continue its efforts.

· "A vote was also passed expressing thanks to the 10 fraternities which have thus far deeded their chapter houses to the university and it was the unanimous opinion of those present that all the other fraternities should follow their example."

The 10 fraternities which have thus far accepted the University proposal are: Alpha Delta Phi, Beta Theta Pi, Delta Phi, Delta Tau Delta, Delta Upsilon, Kappa Sigma, Phi Gamma Delta, Phi Kappa Psi, Sigma Nu, and Theta Delta Chi. The other six property-owning fraternities are: Delta Kappa Epsilon, Lambda Chi Alpha, Phi Delta Theta, Psi Upsilon, Sigma Chi, and Zeta Psi, three of which are definitely listed in opposition to the proposal. ◀

Plates Out of Stock; Reordered

▶ MOST OF THE CENTRES are out of stock in our supply of Brown University plates by Wedgwood, according to John Hutchins Cady '03, chairman of the alumni Memento Committee. Although a new order has been placed, production and shipping delays make it unlikely that delivery can be made before winter. ◀

29

$66,000 for the Fund ◀

▶ NEARLY 4500 BROWN MEN, many of them in the uniforms of the United Nations, sent back $66,011.30 to the University through the 1944 Alumni Fund. The campaign, which closed June 30, established new records for number of contributors, the dollar total and the per capita gift, according to Arthur L. Philbrick '03 of Providence, chairman of the Brown Alumni Fund Trustees and leader of the nation-wide volunteer organization of 350.

The 1944 dollar total was $9,630.70 above the previous all-time record of $56,370.60 set a year ago. The per capita gift went up from $12.95 to $14.68, while the number of givers—4497—was an increase of 143.

"This accomplishment demonstrates the regard Brown men hold for their Alma Mater," Mr. Philbrick said in announcing the final figures. "The alumni gave 17 per cent more than in any other year, in spite of tax demands, patriotic investments, and other undeniable wartime appeals. The alumni knew that Brown was committed to war service more directly and more fully than ever before in her history. On the other hand, they knew that her income was sharply reduced. Alumni giving has therefore done double duty, helping to make Brown's role today an effective one and preserving her solvency for important years to come. All credit for the success of our campaign goes to alumni understanding and loyalty.

"As was the case a year ago, new contributors took the place of several hundred who were preoccupied with military duties. Nevertheless an amazing response came from the men in the armed forces, or their families. All branches of the service, all active theatres, and most training centres were represented.

"We turn this $66,000. over to the University as a gift of free money for its current uses without restriction."

In addition, the Brown Alumni Fund this year received contributions of $1,505.19 to the Alumni Endowment, which permits giving to the capital fund of the University as distinct from giving to current income. The Alumni Endowment, created 17 months ago, now stands at $3,580.02 and added $150. to the 1944 Alumni Fund as income on its capital.

A daily average of $590 for the last 20 days of the campaign enabled the Fund to reach its $66,000 mark. ◀

In Honor of His 25 Years

▶ DR. HARRY W. ROCKWELL '03' President of the Buffalo State Teachers College, has completed 25 years of service in this position. On this Anniversary, his faculty and Alumni Association both presented him with gifts in appreciation of his quarter of a century of service. The City Council of the City of Buffalo has just voted an addition of 42 acres to the State Teachers College campus, which will provide ample facilities for a new Library, an Industrial Arts building, a Home Management house, and two new Dormitories. This building program is to be undertaken upon the completion of the war.

Dr. Rockwell is acting President of the Brown Club in Buffalo. ◀

Time to Stump the Brunonians

▶ FOR THREE WEEKS in a row last spring, the guest on "Information, Please" was a Brown man: S. J. Perelman '25' Quentin Reynolds '24' and Senator Theodore Francis Green '87' All comported themselves like experts. ◀

MAJ. D. O. McLAUGHRY

Red Randall Succeeds Tuss

▶ CAPT. ROY E. RANDALL '28' backfield star in Iron Man days, is the new Athletic Officer at Parris Island, where his Marine baseball team won 20 of 23 baseball games this season, including a stretch of 15 straight victories. "Red" succeeds his former coach, Maj. Tuss McLaughry, who has been appointed to the Office of Judge Advocate. Randall had been McLaughry's assistant. ◀

Dr. Belkin's Inauguration

▶ ONE OF THE YOUNGEST men to be elected as President of an American college is Dr. Samuel Belkin, 33 years of age, who took a Ph.D. degree at Brown University in Biblical Literature in 1935. His inauguration as president of Yeshiva College took place on May 23.

Dr. Belkin studied in Poland, taking the first degree at Grodno in 1928, came to this country soon thereafter, attended Yeshiva College 1929-31, and then came to Brown. He was a student at this University 1931-35, during part of which period he attended also some courses at Harvard and Yale. While at Brown he studied under Professors Fowler, Burrows, Murphy and Casey. His thesis was published in the Harvard Semitics Series as a monograph under the title "Philo and the Oral Law".

Dean R. G. D. Richardson, of the Graduate School, represented Dr. Belkin's Alma Mater and spoke briefly on behalf of Brown University. ◀

Dr. Hill's Half-Century

▶ FOLLOWING the graduation exercises of Classical High School, Springfield, Massachusetts, on June 14, 1944, Dr. William C. Hill, Principal, Brown, 1894, was tendered a reception by the Parent-Teacher-Student Association of the school in the Mahogany Room of the Municipal Auditorium in honor of his 50 years of service to secondary education in New England.

Many prominent citizens and parents, together with hundreds of pupils and former students, assembled to congratulate Dr. Hill on his long record of continuous and outstanding service to the cause of education. Incidentally, he continues as Principal inasmuch as the Massachusetts legislature has passed a law permitting, for the duration, reappointments beyond retirement age.

The Springfield Chapter of the American Red Cross has named him as its chairman. ◀

The Rollcall of Reunions ◄ ◄

▶ ▶ 1879—TWO WEEKS before the other reunions, the Class of 1879 held its 65th annual gathering on June 4. Dr. Stephen A. Welch entertained at his home, with William Ely and Judge Willard B. Tanner attending and posing for the Bulletin photographer drinking a toast to their Alma Mater. Edward S. Adams of Fall River was unable to be present.

▶ 1884—SIXTY YEARS out of College, the Class observed its anniversary with a weekend on the campus with headquarters in the Alumni Guest House set up in Horace Mann dormitory during the Commencement season. A feature was the reunion dinner at the Narragansett on the night of June 19, with seven of the 15 living members present (60 were graduated, according to Col. William M. P. Bowen's record). The group at dinner, which voted another gathering in 1949, chose the following officers: President—Rev. Charles R. Upton of Portland, Me., succeeding Prof. L. Raymond Higgins of Maplewood, N. J.; Vice-President — Augustus L. Holmes of St. Petersburg, Fla.; Secretary— Col. Bowen, re-elected. Col. Albert A. Baker, Edwin C. Gammage, and Theodore F. Tillinghast were also present.

▶ 1890—THREE MEMBERS of the Class lunched at the University Club on Commencement Day: Dr. Harry L. Grant of Providence, who had sent his customary blithe June letter to all the members, Walter W. Presbrey of Providence, and Rev. Hamilton E. Chapman. The Class will be saddened to note that Mr. Presbrey died July 14.

▶ 1891—A MEMORIAL SERVICE at the Class Fence on June 19 opened the reunion in the traditional manner, as a compliment to Fred W. Woodcock of Ashburnham, Mass., and Arthur H. Colby of Montclair, N. J., who died during the previous year. The group then joined the Commencement procession for the march to the Meeting House and lunched at the Hope Club after the Alumni Meeting. The following were present: Joseph N. Ashton of Andover, Mass.; Edwin A. Barrows, Frank L. Hinckley, President George J. Holden, Rev. Charles A. Meader, William Howard Paine, Rt. Rev. James DeWolf Perry, D.D., (honorary member), Rev. James L. Wheaton of Pawtucket, and Everett Cook of Chicago, son of Chester A. Cook. Messages were received from absent members: Dr. Arthur L. Beals of Brockton, Mass.; Prof. Edward B. Birge of Bloomington, Ind.; Rev. Charles D. Burrows of Jamestown; Mr. Cook; Clarence C. Converse of Englewood, N. J.; Rev. Frank G. Cressey of Granville, O.; Herbert L. Dunn of New London, Conn.; Martin S. Fanning; Elbert O. Hull of Bridgeport, Conn.; and Rev. Leo Boone Thomas of Framingham, Mass.

▶ 1893—A CLAMBAKE at the Squantum Club on June 18 was the feature of '93's 51st reunion, with President Edward B. Aldrich as host. Charles M. Poor of Claremont, Fla., and 15 others were present, including Edward H. Weeks, Robert M. Brown, John L. Casey, Robert Cushman, Rev. Edwin B. Dolan, Daniel Howard, Edgar M. Johnson, J. D. E. Jones, Stephen A. Hopkins, Daniel C. Snow, Rev. Elliott F. Studley, George W. Perkins, Dr. William H. Magill, and Thomas P. Corcoran. On exhibition was the Alumni Fund bowl, won by the class in the 1942-1943 campaign. Mr. Weeks, class agent, reported, as did Secretary Brown.

▶ 1894—THE GOLDEN ANNIVERSARY attracted a fine gathering of the Class for the Commencement week-end, centering about the dinner at Agawam Hunt June 17 and luncheon at Chancellor Henry D. Sharpe's the following day. Mr. Sharpe, reunion chairman, received many compliments on the successful anniversary observance. A marine painting by the late Col. H. Anthony Dyer was presented to the Class by his widow and became the possession of Jay S. Fox as the result of a drawing at the Agawam dinner. The Vice-President of the University, Dr. James P. Adams, was a guest of the Class and spoke to all reunion groups at the Agawam Hunt night.
Among those back for the 50th were: Harold C. Field, Fred Tenney, William T. Dorrance, Dr. Israel Strauss, David B. Pike, Prof. Harold D. Hazeltine, Daniel F. George, Herbert D. Casey, Walter D. Brownell, Morton C. Stewart, Dr. William C. Hill, Judge William W. Moss, Rev. Willard S. Richardson, Frank Steere, James S. Moore, Charles S. Aldrich, William C. Bourne, Dr. E. E. Everett, Maj. Clarence H. Greene, William D. Goddard, Dr. Frank E. Lakey, Rev. Charles H. Ellis, J. R. Ferguson, Rev. Dr. J. W. Hill, Prof. Thomas Crosby, Jr.

▶ 1899—FIFTY-FIVE of the 96 living members of '99, an extraordinary record for this year, spent the afternoon and evening together on Commencement Day at the Squantum Club. Howard H. Wilkinson was elected Treasurer to succeed the late Dr. Nathaniel H. Gifford, the other officers continuing as follows: President— Edward A. Stockwell; Vice President— Irving O. Hunt of Wyoming, Pa.; Secretary—Charles C. Remington. Wallace R. Lane of Chicago and George D. Church of Mt. Dora, Fla., came from the greatest distance. Others present: Russell W. Baker, John F. Bannon, Howard C. Barber,

Dr. Samuel M. Beale, Dr. Clarence S. Brigham, Herbert O. Brigham, Rev. Walter B. Bullen, Laurence H. Chace, Julian C. Chase, Wilmarth H. Colwell, George E. Congdon, Jr., Dr. Charles O. Cooke, Ira M. Cushing, Charles B. Dana, George H. Davis, William J. Duffy Jr., Judge Ralph C. Estes, William E. Farnham, Owen F. Gallagher, Charles I. Gates, George A. Goulding, Alexander S. Grier, Benjamin W. Grim, editor of the reunion newspaper, Clarence H. Guild, Jr., Dwight H. Hall, James G. Harris, Joseph C. Hartwell, Louis R. Holmes, Eddy P. Howard, Charles A. Hull, Severance Johnson, Revere W. Kent, Nathan W. Littlefield, Harry B. Loud, Rev. Antonio Mangano, Ernest W. McKeen, Harold T. Miller, W. B. Norris, Frank E. Richmond of Charlottesville, Va., Laurence M. Shaw, Arthur N. Sheldon, Howard R. Smart, John I. Stubbert, George W. Sutcliffe, George B. Utley, Frederick A. Vose, Judge Charles A. Walsh, R. B. Weeden, Alonzo R. Williams, William W. Wyckoff.

▶ 1900—BREAKFAST at the University Club was reunion fare for the Class in this off-year. It was attended by: Chief Justice Fred T. Field, Arthur L. Perry, Benjamin O. Pillsbury, Charles P. Roundy, Albert L. Scott, Secretary of the Corporation, Dr. Herbert H. Armington, Prof. Charles W. Brown, Mendall W. Crane, Melvin C. Johnson, Charles G. Richardson, Dr. Robert C. Robinson, and Clinton C. White.

▶ 1902—SQUANTUM CLUB was the scene of the reunion dinner June 18, with Vice-President Adams representing the University and speaking. Robert O. Smith, Class Vice-President, was chairman. The group included: J. Cunliffe Bullock, R. L. Bowen, George Burdick, Edward K. Aldrich Jr., Rev. Allen Greene, Frederic W. Greene, Jr., Everett J. Horton, W. C. Hardy, Charles B. Coppen, Lewis S. Milner, Harry M. Paine, Judge Russell W. Richmond, Albert D. Shaw, Frederick W. Tillinghast, Rowland H. Wilson, Warren L. Wilmarth.

▶ 1903—REUNION TRADITION was kept intact with luncheon at the University Club on Commencement Day, attended by President John Hutchins Cady, Vice-President Arthur L. Philbrick, Secretary Fred A. Otis,
—Continued on next page.

▶ ▶ Sgt. Wilcox: a Swift Sequel

▶ OUR LEAD ARTICLE last month described "palm inspection" for the B-24s with which Sgt. E. T. Wilcox '43 had had his training in this country. It has a sequel in word this month that his bomber had been forced down in Switzerland on one of its first raids, and the former football manager is now interned in that country.

In his July Fourth cartoon, Frank Lanning of the Providence Evening Bulletin quoted under the heading of "The Independent Man" from a letter received from Ted by Maj. Edgar J. Lanpher:

"I don't think a person loses his individuality in the Army at all. If he has one, it is as a buck private that he finds it. What is lost in the ranks is the outward manifestation of individuality. To make ourselves individuals in the undergraduate mass, we become Cam Club presidents and football heroes. But in reality that proves nothing of the individuality and self-reliance of soul, for the keys, rings and charms are only proofs that we are individuals in the eyes of others . . . I am almost glad I'm private ASN 11096201. I'm glad that the past is dead. I'm anxious to see myself pass the test. Even at Brown I had a good high school record behind me, a Brown Club scholarship, then a strong fraternity. Here I have nothing but myself. I have nothing to prove to anyone except myself.

"I think I have passed the first lap, at least temporarily. I find a great deal of enjoyment in marching down the road one man in hundreds, with a hundred men behind me, a hundred ahead, a half-dozen on each side—flanked by humanity and all alone. It's a warm, comfortable feeling. It fosters a self-consciousness born of an effort not to become one of the sheep. It's a real triumph to be able to walk by yourself . . . and watch . . . and think." ◄

Robert Aldrich, Harvey A. Baker, Charles E. G. Dickerson, Dr. William O. Rice, and Clarence C. Gleason.

▶ 1904—A PLEDGE of $5000 for Brown was fulfilled for the 40th reunion, held at Agawam Hunt under the direction of President Foster B. Davis. Austin K. Allen of San Francisco travelled farthest of the group: Elisha C. Mowry, C. H. Hobson, Harry Smalley, Asa Lloyd Briggs, William Sandager, Adin M. Capron, Edmund K. Arnold, John C. Heckman, Frederick C. Jones, George W. Cummings, Dr. Frederick A. Coughlin, Edward J. Black, Bernard P. Raymond, Charles E. Casey, Howard F. Esten, George L. Spencer, Robert W. Mawney, Everard Appleton.

▶ 1905—A TRIBUTE to the late Paul C. DeWolf, President of the Class for 20 years, was paid during the reunion gathering at the home of W. Howard Barney and later at the Warwick Country Club June 17. Newton P. Hutchison was chairman for the reunion, with these others also attending: Charles Z. Alexander, George B. Bullock, F. A. Burr, David Davidson, Chester C. Greene, Frank G. Howard, Arthur C. Maxfield, Judge John C. Mahoney, John H. McGough, W. Granville Meader, Charles L. Robinson, Frederick Schwinn, Frederick B. Thurber, Thomas Webb, Raymond W. Seamans, Dr. Theodore C. Hascall, Ralph D. Kettner, Dr. Niles Westcott.

▶ 1906—A DOZEN of the Class dined at the Narragansett Hotel: President C. Douglas Mercer, Secretary Elmer D. Nickerson, Treasurer Albert W. Claflin, Percy Shires, Dr. Prescott D. Hill, Dr. Peter P. Chase, E. Raymond Walsh, William G. Winsor Jr., A. Brintnall Tingley, Rev. W. Douglas Swaffield, Arthur C. King, Wesley F. Morse.

▶ 1907—TELEGRAMS of best wishes were sent from the reunion at the University Club June 18 to the following members of 1907 in military service: Maj. Clarence W. Way, Capt. Griffith E. Thomas, USN, Comdr. Charles Hibbard, Col. Frank E. Edgecomb, Lt. Comdr. Francis M. Anderson, and Lt. Col. Donald McLean. A moment of silence was observed for the late George E. Burnham, who died while a prisoner of the Japs. At the dinner were: President George Hurley, Alfred H. Gurney, Harold E. Miller, J. Courtland Knowles, Dr. Frank A. Cummings, Frank Brooks, Victor A. Schwartz, Henry G. Clark, Robert B. Jones, Douglas N. Allan, Frederick S. Auty, Walter C. Slade, Lloyd D. Eddy, Dr. Charles D. McCann, Claude R. Branch, Dr. Joseph I. Grover.

▶ 1908—TOASTS were drunk by the reunion group at the Crown Hotel June 18 to Col. Sydney S. Winslow and Capt. James R. Barry, USN, two classmates in service. Norman S. Case acted as toastmaster; the following were present: Secretary C. LeRoy Grinnell, Treasurer Norman L. Sammis, Dr. Albert C. Thomas, Ronald B. Clarke, Howard R. Newman, James L. Murray, John J. Cooney, Earl C. Bullock, Frank F. Mason, Earle W. Peckham, Howard S. Young, Franklin I. Chichester, Alfred Maryott, and Herbert K. Sturdy, Jr.

▶ 1909—THE CLASS held its informal 35th Reunion this year, consisting of a Dinner at the Agawam Hunt. Forty-five classmates, gathered together under the leadership of Herb Sherwood, perennial chairman of our Reunion Committee, sat down to dinner. Chauncey Wheeler introduced

Jarv Alger who had come down from Montreal. Jarv asked each of the boys who had come from a distance to say a few words. Their reminiscences and Ed Carley's stories were greeted with unanimous approval. Eddie Mayer then showed to an appreciative audience some slides of previous reunions and campus scenes. All left with the firm determination to be present at our real 35th Reunion and to bring with them others who were not able to be present on this occasion. Those present were:

J. Howard Alger, Robert K. Bennett, Clarence W. Bosworth, Frederick M. Boyce, Stuart R. Bugbee, Raymond Buss, Edward K. Carley, A. Manton Chace, Henry S. Chafee, Prof. Robert F. Chambers, Emerson L. Chandler, Newton G. Chase, William M. Connell, James G. Connolly, Moses L. Crossley, William P. Dodge, Henry E. Fowler, Adolph Gorman, Everett A. Greene, Albert Harkness, George Henderson, Edward J. Hollen, Charles E. Hughes, Jr., George T. Huxford, Howard K. Jackson, Arthur J. Kirley, Albert E. Leach, Ivory Littlefield, Edwin B. Mayer, Louis A. McCoy, William D. Miller, William R. Nash, Albert H. Poland, Herbert M. Sherwood, Donald L. Stone, George F. Sykes, Harold A. Sweetland, Selwyn G. Tinkham, James V. Turner, Charles H. Ward, Chauncey E. Wheeler, Dr. Robert H. Whitmarsh, Frank A. Wightman.

▶ 1910—EDWARD S. SPICER was host to the Class at his home in Providence, with a dozen attending: Treasurer Elmer S. Horton, Charles A. Post, J. P. Farnsworth, Andrew B. Comstock, Harold T. Phinney, William J. Dwyer, Albert N. Peterson, Dr. Lester A. Round, Claude M. Wood, James E. Battey, Clinton B. Ward.

Some Faculty Paragraphs ◀ ◀

▶ ▶ CAPT. EDGAR J. LANPHER '19 is Registrar for AAFSAT at Orlando, Fla., "a very pleasant and busy place." He helps run the Post Graduate AAF School and meets many interesting people, including Brunonians, who come and go to and from combat.

1st Lt. R. G. Noyes '21' though busy at the War Department's Bureau of Public Relations, manages to "maintain a constant correspondence with about 120 people." He says, "I am ever more impressed with the excellent writing of the Brunonians: they are well taught by Uncle Bill Hastings and his crew, and of course they have plenty of subject-matter in these parlous times. Those overseas cannot say much, it is true, but they unlock their word-hoards with great skill."

When Prof. Renato Poggoli arrived at Ft. Devens as a private in the Army, they were impressed that he can read 20 languages and speak seven fluently. An Associated Press story recalled that, before he came to this country, he had graduated from the Italian OCS at Salerno and served his compulsory tour of duty in that area, which was considered impregnable.

Bernard A. Hoban, former member of the Brown football staff, is looking forward to his return to coach the sport at the University of Mexico. Last year his team was defeated only by the celebrated Randolph Field eleven. He gave a 15-minute pre-game radio interview in Spanish each week, too.

▶ 1913—INFORMALITY was the order for the off-year reunion at Agawam Hunt, with Duncan Langdon, Class President, in charge. The group included: Prof. Leighton T. Bohl, Preston F. Arnold, Francis P. Davis, Carleton D. Morse, Russell W. Field, Dr. Samuel Kennison, James H. Readio, Jr., C. E. Woodward.

▶ 1914—LETTERS from classmates in the armed forces were read to the 30th reunion gathering at Agawam Hunt held as a token reunion. The first year after the war a major reunion is planned, with all business postponed until then. Present were: Edward T. Brackett, Frank R. Abbott '16, Alexander A. Gardiner, Arthur D. Durgin, Charles E. Brady, S. H. H. Parsons, Charles L. Woolley, secretary, David C. Adelman, Dr. George Rönne, Henry L. P. Beckwith, Dr. Robert M. Lord, Morgan W. Rogers, Leon M. McKenzie, Harold H. Sprague, Sidney W. Wray, Dr. Edward A. McLaughlin, Francis W. Post, Earl W. Harrington, E. G. MacDowell, Albert E. Beachen, Frederic W. Easton, Jr., Melvin E. Sawin, Frederick H. Huling '28, President Robert S. Holding.

▶ 1916—TELEGRAMS went from the informal reunion dinner at the University Club June 18 to the seven classmates in service: Brig. Gen. William C. Chase, Brig. Gen. Francis W. Rollins, Col. H. Stanford McLeod, Comdr. William N. Hughes, Col. Guy W. Wells, Maj. Paul B. Metcalf, and Col. Burton L. Lucas. Fifteen attended the dinner: Charles J. Hill, Franklin C. Smith, Prof. C. Emanuel Ekstrom, Rep. Leon W. Brower, Harry H. Burton, John W. Moore, secretary, Thomas H. Donahue, Jr., John B. Dunn, treasurer,

—Continued on next page.

Maj. Norris W. Rakestraw is commander of the crack Rhode Island Wing of the Civil Air Patrol, which he helped organize a couple of weeks after Pearl Harbor. He does this all on top of a heavy teaching schedule in chemistry.

Cordially caricatured in Frank Lanning's portrait series in the Providence Evening Bulletin, June 15, Dr. Bruce M. Bigelow '24' Dean of Students, was presented as an outstanding Rhode Islander "Brightening His Corner." "He is known as the 'humanizer' on the hill, a title of which he must be justly proud," said the accompanying citation. "All his acquaintances affectionately call him by his first name. It would seem factitious to do otherwise. His sense of humor is exquisite and his disarming friendliness surely gives the college entrant a warm first impression of the school." At the annual dinner of the Providence Brown Club, Dr. Bigelow had said that the test of a university is its product. Lanning's comment: "Bruce Bigelow is a product of Brown University. No college can boast a finer example."

Prof. Joachin Wach represented the New England region at the National Intercollegiate Christian Conference at Lake Forest, Ill., this month.

James H. Case, Jr., Secretary of the University, has been promoted to Lt. US-NR. He is executive officer of the V-12 unit at Howard College, Birmingham, Ala.

◀

John B. Cashman, Francis J. O'Brien, Newton P. Leonard, Francis J. Brady, William A. Graham, president, Frank A. Abbott, Steward T. MacNeill.

▶ 1919—LARGEST of all 1944 reunions was that of the 25-year Class, at Squantum. The company: Samuel Temkin, J. C. Scott, Rufus C. Fuller, Jr., Webb W. Wilder, Standish Howland, William E. Parmenter, Arthur J. Levy, Roger T. Clapp, William M. McSweeney, Hartley F. Roberts, Maurice Bazar, William E. Boyle, Alexander T. Hindmarsh, Stanley H. Mason, John W. Haley, reunion chairman, Sidney McCormick, James B. Corey, Thomas F. Black, Jr., Fred B. Perkins, Charles Bolotow, Daniel Robinson, Earle A. Phillips, Solomon Tannenbaum, Rev. Robert L. Weis, H. Raymond Searles, Dr. George H. Gildersleeve, Louis Smith, W. Chester Beard, Hugh Robertson, William Albrecht, Jr., of Takoma Park, Md., William Moss, James S. Eastham, Edwin M. Murphy, James J. Walker, Philip E. Scott, Ernest E. Nelson, Earl A. Phillips, James A. Pierce, William M. Fraser, Jacob J. Putnam, James L. Jenks, Jr., Glen B. Burt, Malcolm E. Carder, Willis B. Downey, Ralph R. Mullane, Marvin W. Ray, William E. Wheeler, Emilio N. Cappelli, Jacob I. Cohen, F. Richmond Allen, Everett R. Cook of Winnetka, Ill., C. Lincoln Vaughan, Jr. Lt. William H. Edwards USNR, Harold R. Moulton, Charles H. Huggins, Jr., Major S. A. Fox of Martinsburg, W. Va., and Dr. Joshua H. Weeks.

▶ 1923—ALTHOUGH one of their two hosts was in the South Pacific, the Class continued its series of Commencement morning breakfasts as guests of Lt. Col. William B. McCormick and J. D. E. Jones, Jr., at the University Club. Honor guest was Lt. Harvey S. Reynolds, USNR, returned from carrier duty in 10 engagements in the Pacific. Others present were: E. John Lownes, vice-president; W. Chesley Worthington, secretary; Dwight K. Bartlett, Jr., Prof. Clarence E. Bennett, Joseph S. Eisenberg, C. Arthur Braitsch, Nathaniel B. Chase, Lawrence Lanpher, Dr. Wallace Lisbon, Theodore R. Jeffers, Ronald B. Smith, and Robert G. Inman '24.

▶ 1924—NEAREST to the usual style of reunions was the 20th of 1924, held overnight at Cold Spring House, Wickford. Citation of Quentin Reynolds, "Brooklyn's bard of the beachheads," as their "Man of the Year" was a feature of the Class meeting, at which the following officers were also elected: President—Robert H. Goff, who succeeds Joseph W. Nutter after the latter's 21 years in office; Secretary—Philip A. Lukin, 2nd, New York; Treasurer—Earle C. Drake, Syracuse; Executive Committee—Mr. Nutter, Dr. Bruce M. Bigelow, Denison W. Greene, Mr. Reynolds, and John J. Monk of Chicago.

The citation of Reynolds especially commended his "inestimable contributions to Allied unity and mutual understanding, thus quickening the march to Inevitable Victory." He "has gone far but changed little from the Quent of happy college days," the citation concluded. "The measure of the man is the esteem in which he is held by premiers, kings, and generals, as well as by his colleagues and the Allied warriors whose dangers and hardships he has shared, in getting his story when and where the story was happening." It described the field of Reynolds' reporting and his skill in revealing to millions of Americans the meaning of war, the character of our ene-

CHICAGO ORATOR: Quentin Reynolds '24 gave an effective, refreshingly different speech as a self-styled "amateur" at the Democratic National Convention. His classmates earlier, at their 20th reunion, had voted him their "Man of the Year."

mies, and the heroism of our comrades in arms.

Among those at the reunion were: W. Irving Reid, Raymond L. Miller, S. E. Wilkins, Jr., E. W. Harlow, Jack Lubrano, James H. Sims, M. L. Berrian, Carleton L. Staples, LeRoy Eisenberg, Robert G. Inman, William H. Schofield, Edward R. Place, Herbert J. Somers, Edward W. Morris, Prof. Arian R. Coolidge, William Fletcher, Jr., Carleton Goff, John F. Cotton, Louis B. Goff, Charles C. Hopkins, Robert F. Rodman, Jr., Dr. A. V. Migliaccio, Warren Sanford, John MacDonald, Carleton Bliss, and William H. Barclay, Dartmouth '25.

▶ 1934 — A COMMENCEMENT LETTER from Class President John M. Gross asked for a poll of opinion, with the result that the 10-year class voted to de-emphasize what would normally have been a major reunion, The first June following we will see a Victory Reunion to take its place and then some. The 10 '34 men who met informally at Agawam Hunt June 16 agreed to stage that Victory Reunion for the returning veterans. The Agawam group included: John R. Lynch, Leslie L. Smith, Carl S. Sawyer, Rockwell Gray, James P. Patton, Charles K. Campbell, Edward W. Thomas, Hugh Welshman, Stephen S. Phillips, Marshall W. Allen, and Bert Shurtleff '22 who entertained the group with his famous expose of professional wrestling.

▶ 1939—FROM ALL OVER the world came 109 letters of regret, and the 16 members who held a modest fifth reunion at the Hope Club paid their respects to the vast majority of the Class who are in the armed services. A welcome-home reunion is proposed for the first Commencement after the war. Class Secretary Richard Goodby and Emery R. Walker arranged the dinner for the following on June 17: President Irving S. Hall, Charles A. Reynolds, Thomas Quinn, Alfred MacGillivray, Howard Brown, Edward Deignan, Ray de Matteo, M/Sgt. Herbert Goldberger, Charles Harrop, Wickliffe Luhn, Stanley F. Mathes, Herbert Rosen, George Larkowich, and Samuel Bogorad of Chicago. ◀

▶ 9 Trustees

▶ ▶ NINE NEW TRUSTEES were elected to the Brown University Corporation at the Commencement meeting of the Brown University Corporation, five of them nominated by the Associated Alumni to sit as Alumni Trustees. In addition to this election, which followed an agreement that the Corporation would seat all five Alumni candidates instead of only two, the following were elected directly by the Corporation: Thomas E. Steere '98 of Providence, Donald S. Babcock '10 of Providence, Arthur B. Homer '17 of New York, and Chapin S. Newhard '22 of St. Louis.

Mr. Steere is treasurer of the Photostat Corporation, president of the Providence Athenaeum, and director of the R. I. Hospital Trust Co. At one time he was associated with the Castner Corporation of Niagara Falls. He is a member of Phi Beta Kappa and secretary of his class.

Mr. Babcock, a member of the finance committee at Brown for many years, is a financial secretary, co-trustee and executor of the estate of the late Senator Jesse H. Metcalf. He is a trustee of the People's Savings Bank and member of its board of investment, a trustee of the Providence Lying-In Hospital, and a director of the Congdon & Carpenter Co. During World War I he was a major in the field artillery.

Mr. Homer is vice-president of the Bethlehem Steel Co., Shipbuilding Division and has been associated with that company since 1919, when he was made assistant to the general superintendent of Shipbuilding Corp., Ltd. He is president of Bethlehem-Fairfield Shipyard, which set the East Coast record in Liberty Ship construction. Mr. Homer, who resides in Harrison, N. Y., was a Lt. (jg) during the first World War.

Senior partner of Newhard, Cook and Co., investment brokers, and President of the St. Louis Stock Exchange, Mr. Newhard was formerly resident manager of Otis & Co. and at other times has been associated with Bitting & Co., and Lorenzo E. Anderson & Co., all investment houses in St. Louis. He has led War Bond and Navy Relief drives there. A former baseball manager and editor of the Herald, he has been active for 20 years as an officer of the Brown Club of St. Louis.

Under a policy now in force, all Trustees take engagement with the understanding that their period of service will be for seven years. Three of the Alumni Trustees will serve for a shorter period, however, since they were chosen to fill vacancies previously existing in the complement of Alumni Trustees.

Charles Douglas Mercer '06 of Brookline, Mass., and Ronald MacDonald Kimball '18 of Chicago will serve for seven years. Jarvis Howard Alger '09 of Montreal and Donald Gordon Millar '19 of Greenfield, Mass. and Larchmont, N. Y., will serve for four years, and Lt. Col. Marshall Nairne Fulton '20 MC, AUS, will serve for three. Mr. Mercer is president of Willcox & Gibbs Sewing Machine Company, New York, and of Willcox & Gibbs, Ltd., London, England. Mr. Kimball is vice-president of the Continental Illinois National Bank and Trust Company. Mr. Alger is vice-president and director of the Aluminum Company of Canada, Ltd., and the Aluminum Power Company, Ltd. Mr.

33

Millar is president of the Greenfield Tap and Die Corporation, Greenfield, Mass., also well known as an international yachts-man. Dr. Fulton, at present on leave from Peter Bent Brigham Hospital, Boston as senior associate in medicine, and from Harvard Medical School as associate in medicine, is the chief of medical service at the Army's Valley Forge General Hospital, Phoenixville, Pa.

The quota of Alumni Trustees on the Corporation has thus been filled—14. one-third of the total membership of the Board of Trustees. Normally two are elected each year for seven-year terms.

The Corporation Meeting

▶ OF NINE newly-elected Trustees, three were present at the Commencement meeting of the Brown Corporation and took their engagements: J. Howard Alger '09 of Montreal, Lt. Col. Marshall N. Fulton '20 of Phoenixville, Pa., and Donald G. Millar '19 of Greenville, Mass. G. Burton Hibbert of Providence and Walter Hoving '20 of New York, elected last fall, were also present and took their engagements.

Others who attended: Board of Fellows —President Wriston, Albert L. Scott, of New York, Secretary of the Corporation, Chief Justice Fred T. Field of Boston, Senator Theodore Francis Green of Washington, Dr. Charles N. Arbuckle of Newton Centre, Mass., Fred B. Perkins and Claude R. Branch of Providence. Board of Trustees — Chancellor Henry D. Sharpe, L. Ralston Thomas, Clinton C. White, Treasurer Harold C. Field, Lt. William H. Edwards, USNR, (completing his term as Alumni Trustee), Judge John C. Mahoney, Albert C. Poland, Arthur B. Lisle, A. L. Philbrick, Sidney Clifford, Dr. Albert C. Thomas, all of Providence; Edwin Farnham Greene, Norman S. Taber, Charles Evans Hughes, Jr., Thomas B. Appleget, Alfred B. Meacham, Wayne M. Faunce, Dr. Charles C. Tillinghast, Rowland R. Hughes, all of New York; Dr. Joseph C. Robbins of Wollaston, Mass.; Dr. W. Russell Burwell, Cleveland; Wallace R. Lane, Chicago; Judge Allyn L. Brown, Norwich, Conn.; Homer N. Sweet and William P. Burnham, Boston.

Elections included the following: Mrs. Virginia Piggott Verney '28 to succeed Miss Margaret E. Carr '17 as an alumnae member of the Advisory Committee on Pembroke College; Mr. Poland to succeed the late Karl D. Gardner on the standing committee on trustee vacancies; Mr. Lisle to the committee on investment; Mr. Hibbert to the committee on comprehensive planning and development of university property to succeed the late Paul C. DeWolf. (The Advisory and Executive Committee had previously named Mr. Burnham for the Athletic Council, succeeding Mr. Faunce.)

Phi Beta Kappa's Annual

▶ RE-ELECTIONS predominated as the Rhode Island Alpha of Phi Beta Kappa held its 115th annual meeting in University Hall on June 17. The officers for the coming year: President—Arthur M. Allen '97; Vice-President—Prof. Robert B. Lindsay '20; Secretary—Prof. William T. Hastings '03; Treasurer—Judge William W. Moss '94; Auditor—George L. Miner '97; Committee members—C. Gurney Edwards '18, Fred B. Perkins '19, Prof. I. J. Kapstein '26, Clarence H. Philbrick '13,

Thomas F. Black, Jr., '19, Mrs. Eleanor A. Goodrich '26, Prof. Robert F. Chambers '09, Prof. James B. Hedges, Prof. J. W. Wilson '18, Elmer D. Nickerson '06, and Roger T. Clapp '19, Prof. Benjamin C. Clough, Mrs. Wilma Robb Ebbitt, and Prof. William M. Sibley were elected to membership in course.

Alumni Election Results

▶ PAUL NICHOLS SWAFFIELD '16 of Watertown, Mass., President of the Boston Chapter of the Eastern Intercollegiate Football Officials Association, was elected an alumni member of the Brown Athletic Council for a three-year term, following general balloting by the alumni, it was announced on Commencement Day. Mr. Swaffield will succeed Raymond L. Smith '14 of New York. He is advertising manager of the Hood Rubber Co., having previously served the company and U. S. Rubber as an efficiency engineer. He has officiated at many major college games and has spoken and written on themes related to both athletics and his profession. As an undergraduate, he played football and basketball, later coaching, teaching, and directing athletics at Colby Academy, Danielson High, Conn., and Leominster High, Mass.

In the same voting the alumni chose the following Regional Directors in the Associated Alumni organization for two-year terms: Rhode Island—J. Richmond Fales '10; New England (outside of R. I.)—Carleton D. Morse '13 of Needham, Mass.; Atlantic-Midland — Dr. William W. Browne '08 of Yonkers, N. Y.; Central—Earl V. Johnson '24 of Chicago; Western—Fremont E. Roper '11 of Berkeley, Cal. Morse, Brown, and Roper were already serving as Directors, while Fales has also been on the Board in recent years.

Modern Idolatry

▶ PRESIDENT WRISTON drew upon the story of the golden calf for his text in speaking at the Baccalaureate Service, Sunday afternoon, June 18. Modern forms of idolatry, as foolish and fanatical as that of the Israelites, thrive in worship of the state under fascism, emperor worship in Japan, and worship of the machine as it threatens America. "It is in moments of

desperate reaction after high adventure . . . when spiritual elevation gives place to moral fatigue that men do things both futile and silly," he said. The worship of the golden calf "occurred close to four mil-leniums ago; yet we live in the midst of the same stupid sin."

"But the machine does not dominate this age," he continued. "Man is in control unless terror or stupidity destroys his capacity to function rationally—or to function at all. Then he falls into idolatry. . . . The way to the Promised Land is not through the leadership of the molten calf." Progress can be found only in the reality that "men are the children of God."

The Chaplain of the University, Dr. Arthur L. Washburn, and Dr. Albert C. Thomas, the Pastor of the Church, also took part in the service. It was followed by the President's Reception on the Middle Campus before Faunce House.

Welcoming Prof. Ducasse

▶ THE BROWN CLUB of Alta, California, gave a dinner April 11 at the University Club, San Francisco, honoring Prof. Curt John Ducasse, Head of the Department of Philosophy of Brown University.

Other guests present were: Professor George P. Adams of University of California, Mr. T. T. Bell of Stanford University. Mr. Nathaniel Blaisdell, '83, President of the local Brown Club, presided. Among the Brown Alumni present were: Dr. T. H. Goodspeed, '09, Mr. Stephen D. Pyle, '10, Mr. Austin K. Allen, '04, Mr. T. D. Woodbury, '03, and Mr. F. E. Roper, '11,

Professor Ducasse gave the Howison Memorial Lecture on Philosophy at Wheeler Hall, University of California, at Berkeley, California, on April 12. He also lectured at the University of Oregon and visited the University of Washington, where he was formerly a faculty member.

The Engineers

▶ TEST PILOT Steve McClellan '23 was the attraction at the annual spring meeting of the Brown Engineering Association, held April 19 at Midston House. In addition to talking on aviation, McClellan had some official Navy movies to show as well. Ladies were invited, and it was a good evening, all agreed.

Dr. Strauss and Hillside ◀ ◀

▶ ▶ IN THE COMPLIMENTS received by New York's Hillside Hospital on its 25th anniversary last month, Dr. Israel Strauss '94 rightfully shared in large measure. "His was the idea of providing the proper type of institution to care for the curable mentally ill person in poor or very modest economic circumstances. The community was sorely in need of just such an institution. No such hospital existed."

As President of the Society of the Hillside Hospital since its inception, Dr. Strauss has seen, first, the campaign of education necessary at a time when mental health was not to be discussed in the open; then the establishment of mental clinics at Beth Israel and Lebanon Hospitals, followed by the first acquisition of property at Hastings-on-the-Hudson, and finally the construction on a 50-acre tract on the old Vanderbilt estate in Queens at Union Turnpike and 263rd St. The hospital is non-sectarian and non-profit, with a record of never having discriminated be-

tween the paying and non-paying patient's treatment. .

Messages of congratulation to Dr. Strauss were received for the anniversary dinner at the Waldorf Astoria on June 7 from President Roosevelt; Dr. George S. Stevenson of the National Committee for Mental Hygiene, and others. Governor Thomas E. Dewey said, "It is heart-warming to learn that the faculty of Hillside Hospital has cured and returned to their normal place in society more than 2000 people." He also pointed out "how much its faculty have added to the progress of psychiatry, since it was one of the first places where electric shock therapy, insulin, and metrazol were tried." Dr. Stevenson said: "We have had many opportunities to refer to this as a model, warranting the attention of mental hospitals throughout the country." A fine portrait of Dr. Strauss provided the frontispiece of a souvenir book.

Brunonians Far and Near ◀ ◀

BY ALFRED H. GURNEY '07

1884

▶ ▶ REV. EDWARD PRATT TULLER, retired Baptist minister, is living in Washington, Conn.

1886

Frank L. Morse, dean of the Brunonians
of the Brown Club of Chicago, informs
us his correct mail address is 27 East 70th
St., Chicago, 37.

1887

Senator Theodore Francis Green mod-
estly assumed the role of prophet when he
predicted in the Senate on the 153rd anniversary of the Polish Constitution that
Poland would rise again "as a great nation after this war, and that it was in the
interest of the world that she did."

1888

"Silver should be restored to a full monetary position and its price pegged to a
constant relationship to gold," said Francis
H. Brownell, chairman of the board of
American Smelting & Refining Co., according to an AP news story sent out last
month. The story went on: "In urging a
return to bimetalism, Brownell said there
is not enough gold in the world to finance
the volume of international trade necessary
for postwar prosperity." Brownell made
his recommendations in pamphlet form,
handy for the experts who prepared the
agenda for the United Nations Monetary
Conference at Bretton Woods, N. H., this
month.

Bishop Louis C. Sanford of Los Gatos,
Calif., was in Reno in May and called on
Judge George S. Brown's widow. She is
living at 405 Granite St.

1889

Notwithstanding the fact that he continues to enjoy excellent health, Richard
R. Martin has retired from the practice of
law in Utica, N. Y., for more than 50
years. He is taking up residence at the
Governor Clinton Hotel, Kingston, N. Y.,
in the Hudson River Valley where he was born
and spent his earlier years.

Francis Burdick has retired and is living at 12 Kay St., Newport, R. I.

1891

We've been privileged to see a copy of
George Holden's paper before the American Dental Trade Association last year in
Chicago, a thoughtful study of "Power for
Permanent Peace," now available in re-
print. He believes a world federation or
a mobile world police force a matter of
"life or death."

1892

Prof. Arthur N. Leonard, retired from
the faculty of Bates, is recovering from a
siege of illness, according to word sent
from Lewiston to the annual meeting of
the Brown Club of Western Maine.

1893

Charles A. Selden has a grandson,
Charles E. Banks, now at Brown in the
Class of 1945 and in the ROTC, taking all
the Navy courses in mathematics and engineering, which, the grandfather thinks,
are a great deal stiffer than anything the
Class of 1893 ever tackled.

Jed Jones' son, Lt. Comdr. Arnold W.
Jones, was a graduate of the Naval War

College who completed training in the
Preparatory Staff Course there last month.

1894

Dr. Harold D. Hazeltine, retired as
Downing Professor of Law, Cambridge
University, England, has changed his ad-
dress to 5 Concord Ave., Cambridge,
Mass. After attending the 50th Reunion
of the Class, he spent a week at Ninigret,
South County, R. I., as the guest of James
C. Collins '92.

1895

From Theron Clark in Los Angeles: "We
had a slight earthquake at 4 a. m. yesterday
(June 13), but I turned over and finished
my morning nap—quite different from the
time of the Long Beach quake when I was
caught in back of a crowded restaurant
while the 10-foot chandelier kicked about
overhead." Incidentally, we underestimat-
ed a bit when we mentioned (in the May
issue) that he had retired as Registrar of
the University of Southern California after
40 years in this work at Brown, Bucknell,
and USC. It actually totals 43 years.

1899

Capt. Gordon D. Hale, MC, USN, is
stationed at Managua, Nicaragua, with the
Nicaraguan National Guard Detachment,
U. S. Marines.

Rev. Walter B. Bullen, retired from the
ministry, is "voluntary business manager"
of Harlem Ashram, 2013 Fifth Ave., New
York.

Frank E. Richmond, chairman of the
board of the Crompton Co., textiles, has
his office at the plant in West Warwick and
his home in Wakefield, R. I.

Lester W. Boardman reports he has retired and is living at 128 Mount Clare Ave.,
Asheville, N. C. Boardman has been college professor and teacher of English literature in different sections of the country
during the past 45 years.

Mrs. William T. Webb, in this country
for the summer, has been good enough to
send us a memoir about her husband, a
special student at Brown from 1898 to
1899. He died June 13, 1939, after an extraordinary international career in civil
engineering. He served in various capaci-
ties during the construction of the Pennsylvania Station in New York and many
new buildings at West Point. This latter
—Continued on next page.

▶ ▶ An Outstanding Success in Track

▶ ▶ THIS third wartime spring season
brought two Bruin teams varying success.
The trackmen enjoyed their best season in
many a year while the baseball nine com-
piled a record of four wins and nine losses.

During the winter months Coach R. K.
'Rollie' Brown '33, now on duty with the
naval reserve, laid the foundation for the
Brown success in spring track. When
'Rollie' left for active service, he tossed
the ball to the Bruin coach-of-all-work
Charles A. "Rip" Engle, who guided the
destinies of the squad during the recently
completed campaign.

The first meet in which Brown took part
was the Greater Boston Intercollegiates
which were held at Harvard Stadium on
May 6. On that occasion, in the words of
Joe Nutter '24, "Brown gained one of its
most inspiring track triumphs of modern
annals and the best in five long years or
since the days of Kenny Clapp, John Mc-
Laughry & Co. . . ." When the smoke
of battle had lifted from the Stadium's
historic track it was clear that Brown
had spread-eagled the field. The final
totals gave the Bruins 75 1/10 points
and Tufts their nearest rival had garnered
only 39 1/10 points. Tufts, it is only fair to
note, was seriously handicapped by the ab-
sence of some of its best men who were
prevented from participating because of a
student prank. Back in the ruck behind the
two leaders came Harvard, Exeter, Boston
College, Holy Cross and Northeastern, in
that order. At this meet 14 members of
the Bruin team scored. Dick Crossley, ace
hurdler, with 11 points, and Bob Lowe,
1944 football captain, with 10, were the
two leading point-makers. Brown men took
first places in six out of the 14 events.

One week later at M. I. T. the 57th re-
vival of the New England Intercollegiates
was held. Here Brown came in third with
25 points trailing M. I. T. and Tufts who
had 32½ and 32 points respectively. Dick
Crossley was again the outstanding Bruin
performer with a first in the high hurdles,
second in the broad jump, and third in the

low hurdles for a total of 10 points. A
week later at Medford the Bruins secured
revenge at the expense of Tufts when they
nosed out the Jumbos in a dual meet 64-62.
Dick Crossley once more the individual
star with two firsts in hurdles and a second
in the broad jump. Dick was closely pressed
by Charlie Tiedemann who rang up a first
in the 440 (this was the first time he had
competed in that event), a first in the 100
and a third in the broad jump.

The 1944 Bruin track season came to a
close on June 3 when Brown swamped
W. P. I. 76½ to 49½ at Providence.
Charlie Tiedemann, Dick Crossley and
Stan Lewis of Brown and Hugo Norige of
the visitors were the stars of this meet,
Tiedemann being high scorer with 13
points. Dick Crossley, the Cranston boy
who now has been transferred to Trinity
under the Navy V-12 program, was the outstanding member of this well balanced
spring team. Dick scored a total of 46
points in four meets and was undefeated
in the high hurdles.

While the Englemen were enjoying this
great success, the baseball team was running into difficulties. Eddie Eayrs '16,
coach of the nine, was faced with many
problems. From the beginning of the season the squad was woefully weak in hitting, there were only two veteran infielders
and a general lack of capable substitutes.

With the situation as it was Eddie did
well. The Bruin schedule consisted of 13
games—eight with college clubs and five
with service outfits. The Bruins broke even
in intercollegiate competition, winning
from Bates, Trinity (twice), and Holy
Cross, while losing to W. P. I., Harvard,
Yale and Holy Cross. There was much
stiffer competition from the service teams,
many of which numbered on their rosters
experienced professional and semi-pro
players. The Bruins won none of these
games, losing to Camp Endicott, U. S. C. G.
of Boston, Camp Thomas (twice), and
Camp Miles Standish. ◀

35

association with the Army engineers eventually took him to Puerto Rico, his first assignment in Latin America. Among the multitude of projects were: pierhead lines, dredging, harbor inspection, removal of wrecks in Puerto Rico; installation of a water system, erection of sugar mills, railroad extension, drainage and sewage system, design of dock and highway bridges in Cuba and Dominican Republic. After service in the States as a Captain, QMC, in the last war, he went to Brazil, where he spent the rest of his life, first as an active engineer, and manufacturing agent in the highway, railroad, and electrical fields. In Rio de Janeiro he was active as a director of the American Chamber of Commerce, a charter member of the Gavea Golf and Country Club, and a sponsor of the American School. In 1922 he served with the U. S. Commissioner to the Brazilian Centenary Exposition. He was an Associate Member of the A. S. C. E. Martha Washbun Murtha Webb, who married him on April 6, 1910, survives him. She will return to take up residence at Estate Consuelo, San Pedro de Macoris, Republica Dominica, in September; until then her address is: 213 S. E. 2nd St., Fort Lauderdale, Fla.

1900

Rev. M. Joseph Twomey is interim pastor of the Baptist Church in Williamsport, Pa.

Throughout Leonard M. Patton's teaching career, the proper upkeep of the physical plant of the public school and the beautification of the school grounds were his hobbies. His efforts, enlisting the co-operation of the students, were so successful that they were frequently commended by the Boston School Department. It was fitting, then, that following his retirement last year from the William Barton Rogers School in Hyde Park, he should be recognized by a special citation from the Massachusetts Horticultural Society and a tribute from Governor Saltonstall. The latter said: "The love of nature which you have inspired will have a lasting effect upon many individuals and upon the whole community." The Society's President, Edwin S. Webster, referred to the civic pride in-

stilled through Mr. Patton's unselfish and unobtrusive work.

George E. Marble has the sympathy of the Class in the loss of his wife, who died suddenly in Worcester, Mass., early last month. The Marbles had observed their 40th wedding anniversary at Atlantic City only a short time before.

1901

Dr. Harvey N. Davis's son, Nathaniel '46 (he's a member of the NROTC Unit) delivered an oration, "A War Ideal," at our June Commencement. And a mighty good one it was, too. Arthur Hays Sulzberger, publisher of the *New York Times* and recipient of an honorary degree, was highly impressed.

"Oiseau de Jouatt-Taillefer", as Bird Taylor signed himself, took great satisfaction in an article in a recent issue of *The Civilian Front*, which cited his Old Hadley, Mass., Committee on Public Safety for prompt work in getting to a plane crash on Mt. Holyoke. He continues as Secretary, the Connecticut Valley Game Bird Ass'n., its activities much curtailed these days, and writes for *The American Field*, as often as not about his favorite Llewellin setters. The *Springfield Republican* recently printed Col. Taylor's tribute to the late Madame Martha G. Dickinson Bianchi, amanuensis of the poems of her aunt, Emily Dickinson. The Colonel lives in the rebuilt Dickinson Tavern of her ancestors.

E. Tudor Gross' article on the First Window Envelope has been reprinted with supplementary notes. It originally appeared in the Collectors' Club Philatelist.

Lt. Comdr. C. Sherman Hoyt, USNR, has been placed on the honorary retired list, having reached the age limit. He had spent 4½ years of active duty as Supervisor of Shipbuilding, USN, at various stations — Stamford, Conn.; Wilmington, Del.; Bayonne, N. J.; and, for the last two years, at Bay City and Detroit, Mich. He had charge of construction of craft that varied in size from small landing boats and motor-torpedo up to larger fleet mine sweepers. Since January he has been connected with the J. G. White Engineering Corp. at 80 Broad St., New York, for

which he has worked on inspection and production methods in shipyards turning out floating equipment for the Transportation Corps, USA.

1902

Associate Justice James B. Littlefield of the new Rhode Island Children's Court began his duties July 1, after being sworn in by Governor J. Howard McGrath. The court sits at the Providence County Courthouse.

After 34 years of teaching in the Paterson, N. J., schools, Everett T. Whitford has retired, and will enjoy his leisure at his home, Warren Places, Glen Rock, N. J., "keeping the weeds out of his garden and giving more time to observing what goes on about him." He will brush up on his violin playing, too, and devote as many hours as possible to music, a hobby of his for years. He's been principal of School No. 6 in Paterson since 1914. He taught New Testament Greek at Brown for a year, did graduate work at Yale, and was superintendent of schools in New Hampshire towns before moving to New Jersey. "Deciding to retire," he told an interviewer, "was the hardest thing I ever did."

Elton M. Adye has changed his residence from Buffalo, N. Y., to 60 Park Place, Newark, N. J.

Fred Gabbi was kept from the annual meeting of the Brown Club of Western Maine because of a session of the Portland City Council the same night. It is seldom that he misses these alumni gatherings.

1903

Charles B. Boland has changed his mail address from Santa Cruz to P. O. Box 123, Los Altos, Calif.

Arthur L. Philbrick will again serve as a vice-president of the British Empire Club of Rhode Island.

Newton A. Reed of Portland continues to see that Brown gets good publicity in the *Press-Herald*, which he has served for 35 years.

1904

Dr. Paul Franklin Clark has rounded out 30 years as Professor of Bacteriology at the Medical School, University of Wisconsin.

Eugene L. McIntyre's sons, John and Bob, are in the armed forces. John, who won his degree on the Hill in '39, is Sgt., AAF, with a bomber squadron in Italy; and Bob '42, is Ens., USNR, member of the June class at Harvard in the Navy Supply Course.

E. R. Scudder is general manager of Jarvis & Jarvis, manufacturers of casters, wheels and trucks at Palmer, Mass. Unable to come down last winter to the library gathering at the time the Robinson collection was opened, he nevertheless offers to send his old canvas football pants. He recalls one memorable occasion when those pants left him in the middle of a game. ("Charlie Huggins sewed the pants up the next day with black linen thread, and the sewing still holds good.")

1905

Frank W. Stephens is living at 906 Cleveland St., Lake Charles, La., an appreciated note from Granville Meader tells us.

State Senator Fred C. Broomhead will again be a candidate for re-election at the polls next November. The Barrington Republican Town Committee renominated him last month.

The Commencement Procession ◄ ◄

▶ THE COMMENCEMENT procession, formed under the direction of E. Tudor Gross '01, chief marshal, and Frederick A. Ballou, Jr., '16, chief of staff, mustered few alumni in the younger classes and was perhaps half as long as in peacetime. But it was a brave showing, with more than a mere bow to tradition. A single band provided the music, but its theme was the long-honored "Commencement March". And the other amenities were observed, too: the march and counter-march on the Middle Campus, the respects at the Van Wickle Gate, the opening of the ranks at the church and back up the Hill. First man in line was Philip E. Teschner of Newtonville, Mass., Senior Class marshal; the last was the Deputy Sheriff of Providence County.

Aides to the Chief Marshal were: John D. E. Jones '93, Byron S. Watson, '97, John A. Gammons '98, Fred A. Otis '03, Denison W. Greene '24, and Kent F. Matteson '28. Aides in charge of divisions were: J. Cunliffe Bullock '02, Arnold K. Brown '27, Brenton G. Smith '11, Henry G. Clark '07

and Dorothy G. Vernet '34. Marshals included: Prof. Robert E. Chambers '09, Prof. Herbert N. Couch, Harvey A. Baker '03, Dr. Albert L. Midgley '01, Albert A. Baker '84, Prof. Albert K. Potter '86; Samuel T. Arnold, Jr., of Providence, Ellis E. Fuqua of Waukegan, Ill., Lewis H. Mammel of Newtown, Pa., and William S. Mullen, Jr., of Forest Hills, N. Y., Seniors; Ruth M. Pearson and Katherine L. Whittier, for Pembroke Seniors; Inez M. Baumgartner for the Graduate School; Prof. C. Raymond Adams '18 and Prof. Norris W. Rakestraw for the Faculty; and Edwin A. Barrows '91, James H. Arthur '97, Henry C. Hart '01, Lewis S. Milner '02, Foster B. Davis '04, Dr. Bertram H. Buxton '04, John H. Wells '09, William P. Dodge '09, Duncan Langdon '13, Robert S. Holding '14, John W. Haley '19, Thomas F. Black, Jr., '19, J. D. E. Jones, Jr., '23, Robert H. Goff '24, Dr. Jesse P. Eddy, III, '28, Murray K. Macauley '29, James P. Patton '34, Charles K. Campbell '34, Richard W. Goodby '39, Stanley F. Mathes '39; Mace-Bearer, Prof. Leighton T. Bohl '13. ◄

Basil B. Wood has rounded out 20 years as librarian of Massachusetts State College, Amherst, and, according to all reports, is still going actively on his chosen way.

Your Class Secretary is "very busy supplying housing for families of the armed services in Providence."

1906

Rev. C. Raymond Chappell is in his ninth year as General Secretary, United Baptist Convention of New Hampshire, with his office at 22 Amherst St., Manchester. He is a member of many boards, including those of Andover-Newton Theological School, Colby Junior College for Women, and is President of the New England Baptist Council.

Dr. Joseph L. Wheeler, librarian of the Enoch Pratt Free Library, Baltimore, Md., contributed a record of "Education Books of 1943" to the April 29 issue of *School and Society.* In addition to the bibliography, he and his associates selected the best of the lot.

John P. Mead is in the Oil Production Division, Cities Service Oil Co., out in Bartlesville, Okla., where his house address is 214½ East 4th St.

Stephen B. Ames is a member of the firm of Kincaid & Co., insurance at 61 Battery-march, Boston. He tells us his son Knight, Brown 1935, is a 1st Lt., QMC, while George H. Brown 1936, served in the Aleutian campaign as an officer in the mountain infantry.

Prof. Edgar S. Brightman is chairman of the Boston University committee set up to study the university in the post-war world.

Rev. W. Douglas Swaffield, D.D., chairman of the American Red Cross chapter in Taunton, Mass., for 16 years, and Wesley F. Morse, chairman of the Finance Committee, give a definite Brown tinge to the activities. In addition R. Frank Brooks '07 has been treasurer for six years and his wife is publicity chairman. The chapter is always among the first to complete its quota on any job.

Henry G. Carpenter is having his busiest summer at Cold Spring House, which he owns and operates at Wickford. He kept his Brown reunion tradition intact by acting as host to the Class of 1924 for its 20th reunion.

1907

Four of the five sons of Samuel A. Steere and Mrs. Steere are in the armed services—a record for the Class, certainly, and perhaps a record for all Brown classes. Capt. Samuel A. Steere, Jr., AAF, is pilot on a B-26 bomber in the European area; Sgt. Kenneth W. Steere, CE, has been in the SWPA since last October; Joseph B. Steere is in the infantry; and Richard B. Steere, just out of prep school, has signed on with the Navy. "I have only one son left," Sam wrote. "He hopes to graduate from Phillips Academy, Andover, next year. . . . My best to everybody whom you may see. I occasionally see Dillon McEvoy in Washington."

Robert S. Curley asks us to use 22 Amherst St., Biddeford, Me., as his preferred address. He and Past President "Spike" Affleck were the '07 delegation at the annual meeting of the Brown Club of Western Maine.

Rev. Merrick L. Streeter, doing special propaganda work for the Government on the Pacific Coast, is now settled at Apt. 11,

3360 Octavia St., San Francisco, Calif. Mrs. Streeter is with him.

William P. Burnham, Alumni Trustee, has been named as a Corporation member of the Brown Athletic Council. If you have any genuine complaints to make about football, baseball, or any favorite sport, you know to whom to address your letters.

Dr. Vernon K. Krieble, Scoville Professor of Chemistry, Trinity College, Hartford, Conn., will begin his 25th year at Trinity next September.

H. W. (Spec) Paine's second son, Bill, is flying Corsair planes in the SWPA. On the official list he is Lt. Harold William Paine, Jr. Bill, you recall, won his degree on the Hill in '41' and was a varsity golfer.

1908

Dr. Bill Browne, head of the Biology Department at C. C. N. Y., was vice-chairman of the National Wartime Conference of the Society of American Bacteriologists, their 45th meeting held in New York City May 3-5. About 1500 members attended. Bill has served the New York City branch of the society as program chairman for some time and has run these large meetings before, including a joint session of the New York and New Jersey bacteriologists. He has lectured widely on "Food Sanitation" under the auspices of the New York Health Department.

Ens. Fred Brown '40 writes: "I've just seen in the Alumni Monthly that Capt. J. R. Barry, USN, is a member of the Class of '08· I had the honor of serving under Capt. Barry recently and admire him very much, as did every man under his command. He was a very popular skipper."

At the 36th Reunion in June, Ben Frost was re-elected President, Roy Grinnell, Secretary, and Norm Sammis was made Treasurer, in case the Class ever has any funds.

Pres. Ben Frost mailed in a second gift to the Alumni Fund, as long as he was prevented from attending the 36th. Good idea, Ben. Hope the rest of the non-attendants do the same!

Les Swain is basking in the reflected glory of Mrs. Leslie, 1930, who has justified her choice as Head of the Northern Baptist Convention. Les is so busy with his chickens, he can't leave his Cape Cod Farm. Smart way to spend his Sabbatical.

Dr. Harry Robbins represented Bucknell at a Post-War Planning conference at Princeton, but sent his greetings to his classmates, at the time of the 36th.

Henry Stacy, attorney and counselor for the N. Y. Central railroads out Michigan way, still smacks his lips at the Memory of the R. I. clambake given the class at the 30th. "Unfortunately I had no son to send to Brown." His only child, a daughter, graduated from Vassar in 1936, and then married a man who was graduated from West Point the same year, now a Lt. Col. in the Field Artillery.

Jim Wilmot is doing a job at the WPB in Washington, D. C., but has hankerings for the Tiverton Scene, where his son-in-law's father represents the orginial settlers there, in the Manchester family.

Harry A. Jager is Director of the Division of State and Local School Administration on the executive staff of the war-time commission, U. S. Office of Education. He is also chief of the Occupational Information and Guidance Service. Last summer he took an active part in the national Institute on Education and the War, helping to arrange the program.

One of the men has showed us an unusual photograph from Bill Bitting which he took of a four-day-old deer, Dolly, before a shrine at 400 Vanderbilt Road, Biltmore, N. C.

C. LeRoy Grinnell, Secy.

1909

"The family is pulling its weight 100%," writes C. M. Whipple from 72 Dr. Ashford Ave., Santurce, Puerto Rico. He is Deputy Commissioner for the U. S. Employees Compensation Commission for the Caribbean district, but it has involved trips, not only back to the States several times since 1943, but also to Central America, South America, Central, East and North Africa, Iraq, Iran, and Palestine. For news of Stuart Whipple, his younger son, see the 1941 notes. Richard is an Ensign in the Navy, transferred to transport service in the Pacific after several months in Puerto Rico. Two grandsons are with their mother in Iowa. Mrs. Whipple (Alma Brown '10) is a Gray Lady serving in the Army Hospital at San Juan.

Frank Wightman is a Civil Service appointee in the Engineering Department for the State of Massachusetts. His address is 14 Calvin Road, Newtonville, Mass.

Ed Carley returned to our 35th reunion. He is Sales Manager for the Ford Roofing Products Company and is located at York, Pa. Ed says that his home address is 190 E. Spring Ettsbury Ave.

Harold Sweetland is a member of the Appalachian Mountain Club Council. He is in charge of the Club's "Excursions".

Prof. T. Harper Goodspeed, University of California botanist, has been calling attention to hitherto unused resources like the "wild rubber" hidden in the stems and roots of rabbit brush. This weed which grows thick on alkali flats and other Western wasteland is a relative of guayule, and its rubber can be harvested in the same way.

Henry Keough operates the National Employment Exchange, Inc., at 30 Church St., New York City.

Prof. and Mrs. Clarence R. Johnson continue to get a fine response to "Thoughts with Wings," which they edited from their favorite poetry, prose, Bible quotations, and bits of humor—selections for meditation, in short. They have been collecting these items for years and finally had them printed for distribution among their friends·

in booklet form. It's had readers all the way from the Italian front to New Zealand. "I've lived at Harvard, at Istanbul, at Los Angeles, and elsewhere," Prof. Johnson wrote recently from Saranac Lake, N. Y., "but it has always been the Brown campus —and not Boston—which has been the hub of the universe for me."

H. S. C.

1910

Harold A. Swaffield of Ludlowe High School, Fairfield, is .President of the Connecticut Interscholastic Athletic Conference. John Pettibone '98' recently retired as principal of the New Milford High School, has been serving as treasurer of the conference.

1911

Rev. Herbert B. Francis is pastor of Union Baptist Church, Montville, Conn., on the Norwich-New London highway on the west side of the Thames river.

Charles M. Franklin reports he has retired and is living at 95 Glen Ave., Edgewood, R. I.

Robert G. Caswell's daughter Margaret (Pembroke '37) had been in England two years as a bacteriologist with the Harvard Unit when she was married (in Morning Chapel, Salisbury Cathedral) to Lt. Mervyn Gifford Lewis, RAF.

S. B. Dishman was seriously ill at the Good Samaritan Hospital, Lexington, Ky., when John A. Anderson had a letter last month. Dishman has been in the Veterans' Administration in Louisville and Lexington for 25 years.

The program of the Second Annual Meeting of the American Geriatrics Society, held in New York June 8-10, reveals that Edward B. Allen of White Plains gave the concluding paper of the sessions on "Functional Personality Disorders in the Aging." He also discussed two other papers on occupational therapy and geriatric practice. As chairman of the program committee, Dr. Allen was responsible for the success of the meeting and was re-elected to that post, in addition to the office of 2nd vice-president and one of the three executive committeemen.

1912

Rev. William L. Phillips, rector of St. Stephen's Episcopal Church, Plainfield, N. J., is in Tucson, Ariz., for rest and physical rebuilding. He hopes to come back to his duties next fall.

Dr. W. Randolph Burgess, Vice Chairman of the National City Bank of New York, was the chief speaker at the 26th annual meeting of the District Bankers' Association in Washington last month. His topic was "The Banks and Government Finance." Rather late in the day we've seen a copy of the editorial in the New York Herald Tribune based on Randy's earlier discussion of the "inflation gap." At the time he had felt "the financial behavior of the great bulk of our people has thus far been characterized by common sense." The commentator, remarking that Dr. Burgess has "the saving grace of human understanding . . . and realizes that economics consists of a good deal more than algebraic formulae." The economist's statement notwithstanding, the writer thought public spending could get out of hand quickly if people were persuaded that present values of money or property were headed for drastic changes.

Nicholas Mumford's son takes after him as a swimmer. This spring he won points

as a backstroker in the New England Intercollegiates, swimming for M. I. T., being shaded for the individual title at 150 yards and leading off the medley relay trio.

Prof. Walter J. Emmons has been appointed assistant dean and secretary of the College of Engineering at the University of Michigan. The announcement was made in the second paragraph of a newspaper story, the first one of which said the Board of Regents had approved a budget of $7,800,000 for the University's fiscal year

"ROGER" FOR WILLIAMS. First award for good citizenship and outstanding community service at Providence's "Sunday in the Park" entertainments went to Scout Executive J. Harold Williams '18.

1944-1945. Another clipping showed that Prof. Emmons had been re-elected president of the Ann Arbor Board of Public Works. He's been a member of the board since 1939 and president since 1942. In addition, to his activities as associate professor of highway engineering since 1927, he is secretary-treasurer (and past-president) of the Association of Asphalt Paving Technologists and secretary of the Michigan Section, Society for the Promotion of Engineering Education. His son Richard is a Sgt. at Ft. Bragg. All of this welcome information. from a colleague ("which I am sure he would never send you himself.")

1913

John K. Starkweather completed a year in office in April as Mayor of Scarsdale, N. Y. He was the third Brown man elected to govern Scarsdale, his predecessors being Richard R. Hunter '98' President of the Board, and Arthur F. Driscoll '06' Mayor not so long ago.

His son, James O. Starkweather '45' outdid even the acceleration of these wartimes on the campus when he received his degree at the Feb. 27 Commencement. He was graduated with highest engineering honors and magna cum laude, the first and only member of his class to receive a degree before June. His Navy commission as Ensign was awarded the same weekend, following a fine record in the ROTC at Brown.

Elisha Wattles is Captain of the Connecticut State Guard's cavalry troop, the only unit of its kind in the country, and drills it four times a week. Last time we saw Elisha was at the funeral of Karl Gardner, whose best man he had been. Wally Snell

and Teet Bohl also represented the class that day in Fall River.

Howard F. Parker is in his 32nd year with the American Telephone and Telegraph Company in New York, engaged in consulting and research engineering activities. For news of his son, see the Class of 1944 notes.

1914

After 25 years, Maj. Earl H. Walker, USA, chief of the Price Adjustment Branch, Detroit Ordnance District, has received the Purple Heart for his service in the First World War. For meritorious service in connection with "the engineering features, requirement, and supply of French warfare material," Walker was cited in 1919. In 1932 Congress voted to replace such citations with the Purple Heart, usually given only for wounds in action—and now, in 1944, the medal has caught up with him. The decorating officer by a happy coincidence was Brig. Gen. A. B. Quinton, who is Walker's chief in this war, and who was also his superior in the First World War. Since he has been in Detroit he and Mrs. Walker have spent "several very pleasant evenings" with the Carl Raquets, and have seen Arthur Kiernan '11 and Mrs. Kiernan. "I had not seen or heard from Arthur in 33 years," Walker wrote, and added: "Attended a Brown luncheon recently and met Heinie Selleck '09' whom I have known since I was in knee pants. Hal Soellner '28 is one of my men in this war work and is doing a fine job. . . . It has been a great thrill to come into contact once more with these good Brown men after being so far away from them for so many years." The Walker address in Detroit is 1019 Van Dyke Ave.

Your Secretary records with regret the death in Boston, June 3, 1944, of Earle Raymond Delano, and gives to his mother and other members of the family the sincere sympathy of the Class. Delano's cherished ambition was to be a teacher. But not until he was 52 years old did he win his college degree, an Sc.B. at Boston University, and leave newspaper work to begin teaching at North Brookfield, Mass., High School. He left Brown at the end of Sophomore year, worked for the Providence Journal, and the Newburyport, Mass. Daily News, was a founder of the Old Newbury Studio Players, a vice president of G. W. Worcester Memorial Hospital and a former president of the Kiwanis Club of Newburyport. A Gilbert and Sullivan enthusiast, he produced several pieces by that famous team, and directed and managed many plays in his home city.

Charles Corcoran, a special student with the class, has been with Hub Industries, Inc., doing industrial accounting since the National Rayon Weavers Association voted to disband .in the spring of 1942. Hub Industries, formerly Dowty Equipment Corp., in Long Island City, deals in hydraulic pumps, gear pumps, landing gears, actuating valves, shock absorbers and automotive and industrial hydraulics. Prior to being with the NRWA, Corcoran was with the Cotton-Textile Institute, and was chairman of a commission which studied the hegira of that industry from Rhode Island in 1935. He was in charge of cost-accounting for Fruit of the Loom and predecessor companies, 1921 to 1935, and for United Wire & Supply Co. in Providence, 1919-1921. In the Navy during World War I, he was Rhode Island representative of certain groups finding jobs for ex-service men thereafter. He had been cost accountant for 14 years with Manville-Jenckes' predecessor, purchasing agent of Warren Manufacturing Co., and for a time clerk to Mayor Gainer of Providence. He and Mrs. Corcoran (the former Katherine E. Weeden of Providence) are living at 379 First St., Brooklyn, N. Y. One son is in the Signal Corps, two daughters were still in college when he wrote.

1915

John Alexander is special representative of International Business Machine Corp., with his office at 217 Koppers Bldg., and his house at 224 Lavina Ave., Pittsburgh, Pa.

State Representative Harold W. Tucker, one of the Republican leaders in the Rhode Island General Assembly, has been renominated by the Republican Town Committee in Barrington.

Lt. Comdr. A. W. Anthony, Jr., USNR., and his family now live at 257 Trapelo Rd., Waltham, 54, Mass. Anthony is on special duty at the Quincy plant of Bethlehem Steel Corp., Shipbuilding Division.

William G. Thurber and his family have changed their residence from Providence to 238 Highland Ave., Cowesett, R. I.

Donald Dike was recently elected Third Vice President of the Massachusetts Teachers' Federation, which has a membership of over 20,000 teachers. Don has served for six years as a director of the Federation.

Nothing further from Col. Parker G. Tenney since he wrote last winter. He was temporarily at McCloskey General Hospital, Temple, Tex., awaiting retirement. Previously he had been commanding officer at Jefferson Barracks, Mo.

H. G. Denham was the subject of a write-up in The Standard Oiler (Standard of California) recently. He is now president of California Commercial Company, with offices in the RCA Building, New York City.

John J. Scofield recently attended a National Conference of Regional Rent Executives of the Office of Price Administration in Chicago. As Rent Director for Region II, Scofield holds the line on rent for the Federal Government in New York, New Jersey, Pennsylvania, Delaware and Maryland. His regional office, at present on the fourth floor, will shortly be moved to large quarters on the 59th floor of the Empire State Building in New York. He believes Rent Control 'a measure urgently necessary in wartime to prevent inflationary increases in living costs,' is eminently effective in Region II.

L. S. McLeod, who took his A.M. with the class, takes pride in recalling the pilots he taught in the first World War: Maj. Horace Hickham, after whom the field at Pearl Harbor was named, and Maj. John Mitchel, after whom the New York field was named. Associated with McLeod at Rockwell Field at the time were such men as Maj. Gen. Jimmy Doolittle and Maj. Gen. Edwal Edwards. McLeod continued his interest in aviation after the war, serving as first president of the Cleveland Aviation Club which sponsored the original National Aviation Races. While regional manager of Fokker Aircraft Corp., he worked with Capt. Eddie Rickenbacker, the vice-president. He has been manager of safety and plant protection for Stewart-

Warner at Green River, but takes his civic responsibilities seriously, too.

1916

Rev. George J. Cairns, Ph.D., Professor of Education, Marygrove College, Detroit and Monroe, Mich., has been re-elected chairman of the Executive Board, Association of Catholic Colleges of Michigan, for a five-year term. He is also beginning another year as chairman of the Monroe Recreation Commission.

Dr. Maurice Adelman of Lying-in Hospital gave a clinical presentation at the 133rd annual meeting of Rhode Island Medical Society in Providence at the end of May.

Leon W. Brower, Representative from Cranston in the 1943 and 1944 Rhode Island General Assembly, was candidate for State Senator in the Cranston Republican City Committee last month, but lost by a close vote. Brower's new house address is 1274 Narragansett Blvd., Edgewood.

1917

Lt. Col. Ralph A. Armstrong's searchlights have been an important factor in anti-aircraft defense in the Mediterranean area. He's been back and forth between Sicily and the Italian mainland regularly of late, seeing that these million-candle power beams shine like the good deed in this naughty world. His boy, Dick, President of his class for two years at Central High, Springfield, Mass., is ready for Brown.

Capt. Edward F. Waldron is overseas in the AMG. Ed, an Ensign, USN, in the First World War, had been supervising principal of the Union, N. J., schools for 15 years before returning to military service.

Rowland R. Hughes, Comptroller of the National City Bank of New York, is one of five members of the Committee on Postwar Policy, which came into being as the direct result of a conference this spring over which President Wriston presided. A score of the nation's leading economists attended and urged the study and formulation of federal tax policies for the postwar period. The project is being financed by the Maurice and Laura Falk Foundation of Pittsburgh.

1918

Lt. Col. Malcolm C. Hylan is Chief of the Manual Section of the Maintenance Division of the Army Service Forces, with headquarters in Washington.

He is now responsible for the maintenance sections of the technical manuals of all the Technical Services—reviewing, preparing new manuals, and promulgating policies in general on such works. As a home address he still uses Boulder, Colo., where in peace time he is professor of physics at the University of Colorado.

H. Ralph Gordon has been with The Ohio Crankshaft, Inc., Cleveland, for the past two and a half years. His son, Ralph M. Gordon, is in England with the Hq. Co. of a Tank Bn. "Pete Keough '17 and I will be there at the first post-war Commencement" he says. "How about a golf game? Regards to you and the former occupants of 4 Manning St."

Lt. Col. Zenas R. Bliss is attached to Hq, 3rd AART Bn., Camp Stewart, Ga. His son Zene is down there with him as a private.

Rev. Earl H. Tomlin has begun his new duties as Executive Secretary, Rhode Island Council of Churches. He and Mrs. Tomlin were recently guests of honor at a dinner and reception given by the congregation of Calvary Baptist Church, Providence, of which Earl was pastor for 16 years.

Your Class Secretary (Maj. Walter Adler, CAC) is in Washington as a member of the Staff and Faculty of the Army Industrial College. Before going to this post, Walt took a special course in war contracts at the JAG's School, Ann Arbor, Mich.

Norman L. Keller is Vice-President and Assistant Treasurer of Hosiery House, Inc., New York, and Secretary-Treasurer of Chalfont Hosiery Mills, Chalfont, Pa. Norm is living in Doylestown, Pa., at 100 East State St.

Mark Farnum's football reminiscences ran serially in the Hartford Times early this spring, with lively Rose Bowl anecdotes and bits about Robeson, Pollard, Robbie, the Carlisle Indians, and others. "Strolling Through Memoryland" was the title of the series with Staffman Rip Blevins assisting. Farnum, now a resident of East Hartford, is connected with Hamilton Standard Propeller Co.

1919

A. M. Dodge is secretary and manager of the John C. Paige Company, insurance, at 463 Congress St., Portland, Me.

C. Lawrence Evans '19' is comptroller of the Dawson Chemical Corp. and lives at 227 Tunbridge Rd., Baltimore.

James Lyon Samson, younger son of Mrs. Bernard Meeker and Henry T. Samson, was killed in action in the landings on Saipan June 15. The father received letters and telegrams from Lt. Gen. Vandergrift containing the tragic news a fortnight later. Jim was a Pfc. in the Marines, 19 years old. His older brother, Jack, is a bombardier on a Liberator with Gen. Chennault's 14th Air Force in China. On his 11th mission he had two Jap ships confirmed as sunk in the China Sea.

Marshal Al Hindmarsh was master of ceremonies when members of the Palestine Shrine and others gave a small testimonial dinner to Coach Skip Stahley when the latter got his Navy commission. Other Brown men in the group who spoke were Wally Snell '13' Harry Pattee '06' and Paul Hodge '28'

Col. Chester I. Dennis, USA, "is somewhere in France," his mother, Mrs. M. A. Dennis, has recently written us from Valley Springs, Calif.

When Dr. Luetta Chen, Chinese scientist, was initiated into membership in the Radcliffe College Chapter, Phi Beta Kappa, at a rather unusual ceremony in New York, Ben W. Brown of Rhode Island Alpha and the American Red Cross, was a witness. *The Key Reporter*, the Phi Beta Kappa news magazine, tells of the ceremony in its summer issue.

John W. Haley, named in a recent news story as a possible candidate for the Republican nomination as Mayor of Providence, forthwith issued a brief and emphatic statement saying that he was not a candidate.

Morris H. Brown is up in Whitehorse, Yukon Territory, with J. Gordon Turnbull and Sverdrup & Parcel, architect engineers for the Canol Project.

Francis L. Simons is associated with Crane & Co., paper makers, in Dalton, Mass., where his house address is 78 South St

Fred B. Perkins has been nominated as Moderator for the town of Barrington, R. I., by the Republican Town Committee. Fred lives in Barrington, has his law offices in Providence, and a summer house at Buttonwoods, thus covering considerable Rhode Island territory in the course of his commuting.

Edgar J. Lanpher, registrar at the AAFSAT at Orlando, Fla., has been promoted to Major, according to Dean William K. Selden.

1920

Stanley P. Whipple, former Assistant Clerk of the Rhode Island Superior Court, is associated with the law offices of Claude C. Ball, Providence. Stan and his twin brother, Harvey, still look so much alike that as in college days Stan is hailed as Harvey, and the other way around.

Ray W. Greene, one of Barrington's most persistent golfers, has been named as candidate for the Barrington Town Council on the Republican ticket. The Greenes live at 16 Glen Rd.

1921

Maj. Knowlton M. Woodin, Professor of Biology and head of the department at Norwich University, is on leave in military service, we have learned. Woodin went to Norwich in 1923, the year he received his A.M. at Brown.

William B. Robinson is superintendent of the Pawtucket plant of Stein Hall & Co., Inc., starch makers.

Dr. Frank J. Honan is one of Providence's busy physicians in these wartime days. His office and home are at 95 Governor St. Frank's three sons are growing

fast, and the oldest, Stephen, will be ready for college before many years.

Lt. Col. J. Ashley Greene, just back from active service, was asked to say a few words at one of the luncheons of the New York Brown Club when he turned up with Capt. Gardner C. Hudson '27 and Lt. William T. Humphries, Jr., '40' of the AFTAD. Col. Greene brought all the greetings of the Brown Club of Oregon, of which he is vice-president.

1922

Col. Arthur F. Merewether, AAF, is Regional Control Officer, Eighth Weather Region. He was principal speaker last month at the graduation exercises ending New York University's four-year program of training weather officers for the AAF. The class was the seventh to be graduated. In his speech, Art mentioned "that all-important WOT," and we were grateful to the *New York Times* editor who translated the initials — new to us — into "weather over target."

Albert E. Foster, Jr., is in his second year as northeastern publicity representative for 20th Century-Fox Film Corp., with his office at 115 Broadway, Boston. Al lives at 14 Essex St., Newburyport, Mass.

George T. Slavin is running the Rubbish Pickup Service at 31 Mary Ave., East Providence, 14.

Comdr. Frank B. Littlefield, MC, USN, is on active duty at sea and is getting his mail through the Fleet PO, New York.

President Theodore A. Distler of Franklin and Marshall College spoke on "Our Youth Responsibility, Our Opportunity," at the dinner held in Vineland, N. J., last month to celebrate the 100th birthday of the Y.M.C.A.

Prof. Lawrence Whitcomb of Lehigh University's Department of Geology has been elected President of the Lehigh Chapter of Sigma Xi for the coming year. He wrote of the ALUMNI MONTHLY recently: "It is more important than ever these days of rapid change. You keep us informed so well that I really feel as if I had been back to the Hill."

Blair Moody, who has represented the *Detroit News* and North American Newspaper Alliance in Washington for 12 years, is writing a weekly feature for *Barron's*—"Behind the Washington Curtains." He has returned from a three months' coverage of the European battlefronts in time for the Chicago conventions.

Raymond T. Rich, Director of Inter-American Centres, Office of the Co-ordinator of Inter-American Affairs, in Washington is living with his bride at 2500 Q St., N.W., Washington, D. C.

1923

"Mike Gulian, who enlisted as a Private in the Army at the age of 42, and who was out eight months later through the crackdown of the 38-year age limit, has finished his basic training overseas as a Red Cross man, has his two weeks' practical training in a southern army camp, and if he isn't on his way somewhere by the time you're reading this, it evidently won't be long." Bill Cunningham reported it in the Boston Herald for July 8. The headline writer said: "Gulian Bound to Get Over."

Ray Goodman is manager of the Western Sales Division, Fawcett Distributing Corp., with his office at 52 West Putnam Ave., and his home at 52 Sherwood Place, Greenwich, Conn.

That really is Harvey Reynolds' picture in Max Miller's new book, "Daybreak on Our Carrier."

Artcher E. Griffin is salesman for American Cyanamid & Chemical Corp., working out of Room 1018, 401 North Broad St., Philadelphia and living at 333 Bala Ave., Cynwyd, Pa.

Sedgwick Ryno, personnel manager for *The Fair*, Chicago department store, has been promoted to secretary of the company. Formerly with Bamberger's, Newark, N. J., he has been in Chicago several years.

Maj. Townes M. Harris, USA, asking for a change of mail address to 2809 South Abington St., Fairlington, Va., added: "My best to all my old friends in Providence." His sons, Wendell G. Harris and Townes M. Harris, Jr., USNR, are at Dartmouth. Wendell entered this month under the Naval Aviation (V-5) program, and Townes, Jr., is studying in V-12.

Ed Lincoln has been renominated for the post of Probate Judge for the Town of Barrington, R. I., where he also skippers one of the best beetle-boats in the "Tired Fathers." fleet. He is a member of the Providence law firm of Hinckley, Allen, Tillinghast & Wheeler.

Lt. Pete Simmons, writing to Jack Monk '24 from England, asks: "Do you remember the play you and Frank Hough wrote (which I produced) entitled 'The Bar of Avon'? I thought of you and Frank recently when I visited the spot you were writing about. Found the Bar, too."

1924

Lt. W. H. Butler, USNR, is on duty at Bayonne Annex, Naval Supply Depot, Bayonne, N. J. He received commission in November, 1943, and was in Washington for a short time before assignment to his present station.

Henry M. Bodwell is a newly elected Second Vice-President of Northern Trust Co., Chicago, and is working in the Trust Division. Before going to the bank he had been with Standard and Poor Corp., investments, for 16 years.

Fred Harvey is owner of the Harvey Co., a department store, in Nashville, Tenn., where he lives on Belle Mead Blvd. Fred notes that he has had his name legally changed from Frederic M. Harvey to the simpler form given above.

Douglas C. Pettigrew is receiving, stock and order clerk with the Wellesley Hills Market, Wellesley Hills, and is living at 25 Irving St., Newton Center 59, Mass.

Laurence F. McDermott is on the sales staff of Wyeth, Inc., medicinal products, of Philadelphia. He works out of the Chicago office and lives at 333 North Lovel Ave., Chicago, 44.

Capt. Clarence C. Chaffee, AAF, is the newly appointed Special Service Officer, AAF Redistribution Station No. 2, Miami Beach, Fla., promoted a week after his arrival from Scott Field, Ill. The station receives combat veterans and determines their next assignments by means of medical tests and classification interviews. While the veterans are at Miami Beach, Chafe has full charge of the athletic, recreational and off-duty educational program designed to help them to relax while "undergoing reassignment processing."

Maj. Henry Howard, 2nd, AAF, is Director of Administration, Walla Walla, Wash., Army Air Field.

"Certainly wish I could have been present at our 20th Reunion," wrote Davy Jones last month, noting his new house address, 829 Wisconsin Ave., Oak Park, Ill.

Robert H. Cowing sets himself as Sp (A) 1/c, USNR, and gives his current address as Treasure Island Gym, San Francisco. Bob has been a publicity director and free lance writer.

Capt. Harold Hassell is now detailed to the Ordnance Department, with offices in the Mercantile Building, Rochester, N. Y. He was previously in the Corps of Military Police.

Dr. George H. Hunt is Chief of Surgery at the U. S. Marine Hospital, Louisville, Ky., having been transferred from San Francisco last December. "My tenure here is of course indefinite, depending upon the needs of the Service—as an example of the possibilities, my predecessor is now in the South Pacific on a Coast Guard ship. My grade is Surgeon, U. S. Public Health Service. That has nothing to do with my doing surg-

"A FEW PILOTS display understandable interest in European geography," was the caption on this snapshot from a fighter bomber squadron in England. The "lecturer" is Capt. Mahlon Meier '24.

ery but is our grade corresponding with Lt. Comdr. or Maj., but we don't actually have either of these titles. As a matter of fact, the officers of the Public Health Service still think that Doctor is a pretty good title, and that is used for all grades up to and including Dr. Parran."

Gordon Smith, who coaches the team at M. I. T., is the new president of the New England Intercollegiate Swimming Association. The Brown coach, Joe Watmough, is vice-president.

Joe Nutter's article on the treasures of the new Edward North Robinson Collection in the John Hay was the feature of a recent issue of Books at Brown. He challenged well the idea that the literature of sport does not match either spectator's or athlete's interest.

Capt. Frank Hough of the Marines had been in the tropics for six months when he wrote Jack Monk in appreciation of the latter's Chicago Brown Club house-organ The Brown Derby. "This particular Tropical Paradise which we occupy now we had the satisfaction of taking over personally from one of the Axis Powers, which, because of the vagaries of censorship, we are not permitted to mention by name. No doubt this seems an odd way for a guy to be spending his middle age, but it's positively a relief after the Battle of Washington. It seems to agree with me: have lost 20 pounds and feel better than in years. Some day after this war is over, I'm going to do a bit of research to determine what became of all the food, liquor, etc., which civilians are being obliged to do without; God knows, we're not getting it here. In fact, I haven't had a drink since 9 October, though they have given us fresh meat four times now in the past 11 weeks. And we had two eggs—the old-fashioned kind, with shells on 'em—early in February."

1925

Charles H. Cuddeback, Vice President of Douglas L. Elliman & Co., real estate, New York, has recently bought a house in Scars-

dale, N. Y., which already has a large Brown colony. Charlie writes: "My son Alva, class of 1947, is now in the Marines. I think I am the only '25 man with a son in service." His Scarsdale address is 21 Clermont Rd.

Herbert A. Campbell reports he was best man at the wedding Jan. 12, 1944, of Sgt. Elon J. Notley '26, USMCR, to Miss Charlotte McK. Shields of New York at Forest Hill Presbyterian Church, Newark, N. J., and that he was host to Arthur Nelson '24 and Mrs. Nelson at the Campbell summer cottage at Lake Hopatcong on May 20. Herb's mail address is 601 Parker St., Newark, 4.

Norman O. Tietjens is an attorney with the U. S. Treasury Department in Washington, Kent Godfrey '26 tells us. Norm and Kent recently had lunch together in Washington and talked of old times at Brown.

Marshall G. Ferguson has changed his address to RD No. 1, Niantic River Rd., Waterford, Conn.

This will confirm our May report that Ben D. Roman will go to Phillips Exeter Academy Sept. 1 as a member of the Latin Department. He has completed 16 years of service in the public schools of Brookline, Mass., lately as principal of the John D. Runkle School. Thus he returns to the private school field where he started his teaching career directly after graduation.

1926

Kent Godfrey is doing advertising work for the Chesapeake & Potomac Telephone Co., Washington.

Quincy Adams is with the U. S. Department of Commerce in Washington.

Maj. Willard Potter, AAF, writes his new assignment is with Unit Hq Section, Scott Field, Ill.

Staff Sgt. Elon J. Notley, USMCR, is on duty at the Marine Barracks, Navy Yard, New York, so Herbert A. Campbell '25 tells us. Of Herb's report of Notley's wedding, please read the '25 chronicle in this issue.

"An intelligent and unpretentious report on the war in the South Pacific and how the Americans there are reacting to their dangerous and difficult life," a *New York Herald Tribune* reviewer called Duncan Norton-Taylor's book, "With My Heart in My Mouth," which Coward-McCann brought out last month. "He is truly a war correspondent in only one part of the book—his excellent and skillful description of a night surface engagement in the Kula Gulf. Throughout most of the remainder of the book, however, Mr. Norton-Taylor is much more interested in the impact of events on minds and personalities than with exciting accounts of naval battles."

Emery B. Danzell has been indorsed by the Warwick, R. I., Republican City Committee as a candidate for the Warwick School Committee next fall. Emery's running mate will be Carleton W. Merritt, also well known as a coach and basketball official; so their campaign should have a strong sports appeal.

New advertising manager of the *Cleveland News* is Gerald F. Disney, promoted to succeed Leo P. Doyle, now business manager of the newspaper. Disney, local advertising manager for 12 years, was previously advertising manager of the W. B. Davis Co. and, before coming to Cleveland, advertising salesman on the *Rochester Journal-American*.

Maj. George L. Cassidy is overseas with the AMG. He stopped off in Providence during the short furlough that followed his graduation from the military Government School in Virginia.

1927

"Spent about 15 months in North Africa and now have spent several months in this sunny (at times) Italy," wrote Capt. Richard E. Barnes, DC, USA, in a V-mail letter dated May 30. "Am living in a third class Italian passenger car, having knocked out the partitions separating sections to make me a nice little room of about 6½ feet by 10. Very cozy and a lot better than it may sound. Still keeping busy, but have managed to get in a couple of trips through the country and find it very beautiful. Last Sunday had dinner at the home of an old farmer who spent 14 years working in the Boston shops of the Boston & Maine R. R." Dick, who carries his dental equipment in a compact unit, is with the 755 Ry Shop Bn, APO 400, c/o Postmaster, New York. "Please change my rank and APO," he ended, "as I don't want any delays in getting my ALUMNI MONTHLY. There's never an issue that I don't scour each and every line to try to locate some Brown man near me."

Edward T. Richards has completed his fifth year as a member of the National Executive Council of Psi Upsilon. What with his fraternity and Brown activities, Ed's leisure time is well occupied. He took a prominent part in the recent War Bond drive, too, organizing the East Side canvass in Providence.

Capt. Ralph C. Taylor has completed his fifth year on the Faculty of Norwich University as Assistant Professor of English. He lives at the Weather Bureau on the campus at Northfield, Vt., but, we are assured, is in no way responsible for the weather or for reports thereon.

Stanley T. Adams is a product engineer at the Electrical Cable Works, American Steel and Wire Co., Worcester, Mass., where he lives at 96 Brookline St.

Variety reported last month that Robert W. Buckley, CBS network salesman in Chicago, had been "upped" to assistant sales manager of the network's western division, effective July 1. "Buckley, who formerly had run the N. Y. office of Bill Rambeau, station rep, was with CBS in N. Y. for three years. Promotion was in line with the network's policy of strengthening the western division sales staff." Bob is a regular at the luncheons of the Chicago Brown Club.

Over in Rhode Island Hal the other day and saw some copper ore samples sent back from the Cananea Consolidated Copper Co. of Mexico by Dr. Arthur Cleaves, formerly a member of the department at Brown.

Though he has been promoted to Captain, Roger H. Case's activities in the Office of the Finance Officer, USA, at 80 Federal St., Boston, continue the same.

1928

Candidate for Rhode Island Secretary of State on the Republican ticket next fall will be Thomas J. Paolino, who has been active in party affairs since leaving college and who was the original Willkie booster in his home sector.

Paul H. Hodge, President of the Brown Club of Providence, was guest at the annual dinner of the Harvard Club of Rhode Island and the Harvard Clubs of Fall River, New Bedford, and Taunton at the Agawam Hunt, East Providence, June 21.

Major Ewing W. Brand (recently promoted) is air inspector at an VIII Air Force Service Command station in England where battle-crippled bombers are renovated. From 1936 to 1942 Maj. Brand was employed by the Motor Sales Company of Baltimore and was vice-president when he left to enter OCS in 1942. Commissioned 1st Lt. in August of that year, he later attended the AAF Engineering School at the AAD, Sacramento, and the Pratt and Whitney plant engine school. He's been in England since early in 1943, leaving his wife behind at 9040 Byron Ave., Miami Beach, Fla.

Speaking at the send-off dinner to Skip Stahley late this spring, Paul Hodge said:

"I have been associated with Brown football since 1924, and I feel that no Brown coach in that time, not even in the case of the '26 Iron team, got as much from the material as Skip Stahley did from last fall's team.

Byron S. Hollinshead is at Cambridge for 10 months as a member of Harvard's University Committee on the Objectives of a General Education in a Free Society.

It's Maj. Dixwell Goff, FA, now, Dick having been recently promoted. He's out in the SWPA with the 43rd Division and is making a fine record as Battalion Operations and Training Officer.

1929

Maj. Walter C. Fisher of the Signal Corps was quartered in an English castle, the last we heard. His wife and their two children are living on Long Island. Anthony, the baby, had his first birthday April 23, which is Cy's birthday, too.

Edson R. Rand has completed his first year as Bursar of Teacher's College, Columbia, and now has the additional title and duties of Acting Comptroller. His office is in Russell Hall, 525 West 120th St., New York 27.

Rev. Charles R. Bell, Jr., preached the baccalaureate sermon for the 106th graduating class of Judson College in Alabama last month. Bell, pastor of Parker Memorial Baptist Church, Anniston, is one of Alabama's prominent younger ministers.

Lt. W. W. Elton, USNR, is a member of the NTSI staff, on duty at the Hollywood Beach Hotel, Hollywood, Fla., to which he went last month from the pleasant confines of Rye, N. Y.

F. Charles Hanson's new rank is Comdr. USNR. His mail address continues to be 5 Olympia Ave., North Providence, R. I.

Capt. Bradford A. Clark, FA, was at Borden General Hospital, Chickasha, Okla., when he sent in his alumni ballots the middle of last month.

Stephen W. Tourtellot is at Camp Endicott, Davisville, R. I., in the civil service.

Unlisted previously on our military roll is the name of 2nd Lt. George W. Thorp, Jr. (Best address is his father's—155 Arnold Ave., Edgewood, R. I.) Harold E. Miller '07 was good enough to point out our omission.

OUR SENIOR MARINE is Lt. Col. H. S. Mazet '26, executive officer of the USMC Air Station, Mojave, Cal., and author of note. (Official U. S. Marine Corps photo.)

We heard in May from Pvt. Robert P. Montague, one of the first Pre-Pearl Harbor fathers inducted in Southbridge, by the very board which he had served so well as Government Appeal Agent. Although he was at the Anti-Aircraft Replacement Training Center in Camp Stewart, the future as to the second part of his basic was very vague.

As far as Capt. Samuel W. Bridgham, MC, could go was to say he was "somewhere in England." He follows these class notes avidly, he says, as well as news of the campus.

University Club News of Boston says in its current issue: "Jack Nilan is quite the Hollywood producer—and can he pick the Pin-Up Girls. He did a grand job of the recent show put on by the American Mutual Insurance Company. By popular demand it has played to several servicemen's audiences."

Lt. Comdr. Al Cornsweet is stationed at Hart's Island outside of New York, according to Harold K. Halpert '28.

Fred Bentley is based at Fairbanks, Alaska, Norman Arnold '30 writes.

1930

Lt. Herman O. Werner, Jr., USNR, noted his new address, 112 Queens St., Chestertown, Md., when he sent his check for the Alumni Fund to your correspondent the middle of last month.

Woodworth L. Carpenter has become a member of the good Brown law firm of Hinckley, Allen, Tillinghast & Wheeler, Industrial Trust Bldg., Providence, with which he has been associated since admission to the Rhode Island bar.

Capt. David C. Anthony, Jr., brought his bride to Rhode Island this month during his furlough from Camp Belvoir, where he commands a Service unit. This has

been his post since commissioned, and for his first three months he was placed with the Provost Marshal's office and rode six to eight hours a day as a mounted officer in the M. P.'s.

J. Oscar Clark came in with one of his usual whimsies by remarking that it took a request for the green stuff to get him to write to me. That's an awful reputation that I am developing. Oscar is now with the Air Transport Command and his address is Captain J. O. Clark, Jr., Air Transport Command, Battle Creek Hotel, Miami Springs, Florida.

Dave Alper in response to a request to help out on the Alumni Fund, reported that he is not only working and running his own business, but is working on a swing shift six nights a week in a war plant. As he puts it himself, "you can readily see I have little spare time."

In response to the same plea, Norm Arnold reported that he is busy traveling through South Carolina, Georgia, Alabama, and Tennessee. His family is fine and he said that the two redheads are real "rebels" now. Norm is apparently becoming a real going southerner because he states he expects "to live and die in Dixie."

In my own peregrinations through New England, I landed in Brockton where I found C. Hazard Beckford—Tubby to you, holding forth in his usual style. He said business is good between repairing automobiles and trying to run the speaking engagements for the Rotary. He is a busy man and his new address is 810 Belmont Avenue, Brockton, Mass.

Two of the members of the Class have suffered the loss of their fathers this month. Woody Carpenter's father passed on early in October and Don Kaffenburgh's father died recently. The sympathy of the Class

has been extended to both Woody and Don.

2nd Lt. Edward L. Sittler, Jr., was with an Ordnance Training Regiment, Aberdeen Proving Ground, Md., when we had a card from him the first week in May.

Gil Rich, writing from Sampson, N. Y., reports a change in rating from AS to PhM 3/c—which any sailor in the Class, sea going or otherwise, will be able to translate with ease.

The cornerstone of the Raymond Blank Memorial Hospital, the gift of Ray's parents, was laid in Des Moines, Ia., Sunday, May 14. A box placed in the cornerstone included photographs of Ray, a copy of a thesis he wrote while at Brown, newspaper stories concerning the hospital, copies of several medical journals and a program of the cornerstone exercises.

George C. Hatch, Jr., reports he is with Slatersville Finishing Co., Slatersville, R. I.

Lt. A. H. Roitman, USNR, has the sympathy of the Class in the loss of his father, Barnet Roitman, founder and treasurer of Roitman & Son, Inc., furniture dealers, who died at his home in Providence, May 24.   HAL CARVER

1931

"Those air bombs or doodlebugs come over occasionally but are a farce as a weapon of war," writes Jerome S. Anderson III, S2c. He has been a driver for a commander (Yale, 1927) and finds it an ideal way to get to know England—"a dry-land sailor, you see, which is strange for a fishing-town lad .... but over here the soldiers are going to sea in their amphibious gear, and we sailors are being sent ashore—at least to a limited degree. "It's morning," he concludes, "and the bombers above, headed for Hitler's realm shake this Quonset hut with their roar. It's grand to see them."

Stan Nickerson, with the Public Relations Dept. of N. W. Ayer & Son in New York, shares an office with Phil Rogerson '40. Stan's first job was to work on the centennial of the telegraph.

Lt. Joseph A. O'Neil, D-V(S), USNR, was a graduate last month of the preparatory staff course at the Naval War College's 60th Commencement. Flagship duty is in store for him with the Amphibious Forces.

W. T. Scott, literary editor of the Providence Journal, contributed a fine article on Howard Phillips Lovecraft in a recent issue of Books at Brown, publication of the Friends of the Library. In connection with the current vogue of this "Haunter of the Dark," it is interesting to note that the John Hay has acquired a rich fund of manuscripts and memorabilia about Lovecraft. The writer of weird tales lived just down the hill from the library, at 66 College.

Alden R. Walls has been re-elected president of Phi Kappa Psi of Rhode Island, Inc.

Hillis K. Idleman, principal of the East Hartford High School, sends us this home address: 267 Naubuc Ave., East Hartford, Conn.

Sgt. Stanley A. Pillsbury, who has been in India with the Army Air Detachment, is now stationed in China, according to word received by his father, Benjamin O. Pillsbury '00 of Needham, Mass. Elmer E. Butler '03 of the Boston Herald supplied the APO number which we had been lacking.

Kenneth S. Fisher was promoted to Lt. (senior grade) this spring, according to his family, which reports him serving as executive officer aboard a sub-chaser, stationed until recently in Suva, Fiji Islands.

First-Hand Opinion on India

▶ ▶ "I'VE ACQUIRED much respect for the British as administrators and business men," writes Lt. Milton Korb '31› MC, in India with one section of the Rhode Island Hospital unit. "The tea garden hospitals run by the British for the coolies are often better than our large municipal hospitals and certainly better than most of our State institutions. They've found that it's not only philanthropic but also economic to keep the coolies in good health. Public health measures, such as anti-malarial work, are usually well done, and they look after the pregnant women and the infants. The Indian owned and operated gardens are not nearly as efficient, and coolie welfare is usually neglected. It seems whatever there is good in this country was brought in by the British.

"Despite the anti-British propaganda fed us by the newspapers in the States, one readily appreciates here how impractical it would be to give the Indians complete independence now. It would hinder, not aid, the war effort. The Indians are not yet able to govern themselves, the mass of them are easily led by any demagogue willing to play on racial prejudice. As it is now, it is only the British who now keep them from jumping at each other's throats." ◀ ◀

The alumni ballot at Commencement time caught up with Warren S. Davidson, 1st Lt., AC, at Lakeland, Fla., where he was awaiting a new assignment after almost four months in Panama.

Lt. (jg) James Minicus, "sufficiently settled" at Pensacola NAS, hopes this magazine will start catching up with him.

T/5 George M. Knowles, Inf., is attached to Hq. Co., 2nd Bn., 260th Infantry, which was at Camp Shelby, Miss., when we heard of George's whereabouts the middle of May.

C. E. Roché has been with International Standard Electric Co., the export division of International T. & T. Co., at 67 Broad St., New York, since last September, he wrote in response to a query from your correspondent. "Have frequently seen Dave McMasters, Walt Tavener, Bob Rutan, Elliott Schulz, and Les Eaton, all of '31'," he added. "Have been active with the Verona, N. J., Service Men's Committee, aiding boys in service by sending them birthday and Xmas gifts and raising funds for them, and have been playing with the Verona Players in the Hart-Kaufman sketch, 'If Men Played Cards as Women Do,' which we have had to repeat on four different occasions. Otherwise things same."

Lt. Westcott E. S. Moulton, USNR, is studying at the USNTS (Radio), Alabama Institute of Technology, Auburn. Wecky was previously in the Armed Guard, on active duty in the Atlantic. Whenever he was in port during the winter and spring he played hockey with a New York team. Fact is, last time we saw him in Providence he had his hockey skates under his arm, and was heading for the Auditorium to limber up.

Major Waldo H. Fish, Jr., FA, with the 43rd Division in the SWPA, has been decorated with the Army Bronze Star for his work during the New Georgia campaign. "At all times during this campaign," his citation reads, "he was on duty day and night, resting only during quiet periods. His superior technical knowledge, keen judgment, and untiring efforts were largely responsible for the successful support which his battalion gave to the infantry during the entire operation."

Ralph L. Ainscough is secretary of the Pawtucket Lions Club.

William S. Wilson is Associate Professor of Chemistry at Georgetown College, Georgetown, Ky.

1932

After a successful season as hockey coach at East Providence High School, Tom Eccleston, Jr., has returned to Burrillville

High School, where he will be athletic director, and will coach football, baseball, and hockey. He will also teach history. Sounds like a full program, but Tom doesn't mind.

Maj. Edward R. Squier, DC, USA, is with the 48th Evacuation Hospital Group—the Rhode Island Hospital unit—in India. Ed has been out there 17 months. Mrs. Squier is living with her parents at 468 West Ave., Pawtucket.

Dr. Miner T. Patton (he received his degree of Dr. of Education from Harvard a year ago) is a Lt. (jg) in the USNR anti-submarine service as a staff specialist officer. After training in San Diego he was assigned in April to active duty in San Juan, Puerto Rico. His wife, Constance Candee Brown '30› and their young son stayed behind in the States. Lt. Patton is the son of Leonard M. Patton '00 of Milton, recently retired Boston school principal, and brother of Dorothy Patton Lockwood '23›

Ivor D. Spencer, who has been teaching at the Citadel, has been commissioned a Lt. (jg), USNR and expects to report for training in Florida at the end of the month. Paul Gleeson passed the news along.

We used Bernard Slater's photo in the last issue but did not tell his whole story. After taking his law degree at Harvard, he was admitted to the New York bar and practiced for some time there. He entered the resin industry, however, to become general manager of Paramet Chemical Corp. in Long Island City, N. Y., in 1937 and is now vice-president and general manager of Paramet Corp., wholly owned subsidiary of Libbey-Owens-Ford Glass Co., of Toledo, O. A trade magazine recently referred to him as having an established record as a leader in the industry. A star wrestler and honors student as an undergraduate, he changed his name legally in 1936 from Bernard Spiwak. His residence: 3 Parkside Drive, Great Neck, N. Y. Pressure of business, he says, is "a rather lame excuse" for being out of touch with his class and the Hill.

Within a period of a few weeks last spring, at widely separated points in the Pacific, Lt. Gerald L. Bronstein, USNR, saw Art Bijur '41› Pat Kenny '25› and Fred McCloskey. "When I saw Pat he had just come back from Providence and his stories from home didn't help my spirits any. It was a pleasure seeing Art Bijur, whose brother Bill was active in Sock and Buskin in my college days. McCloskey, who piloted the plane I was on, isn't a Brown man, but he's a native of Providence who attended LaSalle and School of Design."

"One thing that pleases me as I go among college men, whether it be South or West, is the fine reputation Brown enjoys," Newell H. Morton wrote to Dean Arnold. He was a 9L in French Language under the ASTP, studying at the University of North Carolina at Chapel Hill.

Pfc. Raymond Hamilton, with a Signal Service battalion at Warrenton, Va., wrote recently that he was glad Brown was starting to do something about the fraternity houses. "I have yet to see any that present such a poor picture as those at Brown," he says.

1933

This was the second year, on request, that we've sent to Maj. John Flemming overseas the date of Commencement. He wrote June 11: "Felton (WO Arthur P. Felton '34› a fellow Phi Gam) and I will probably do our best to celebrate in due style. This is his 10th anniversary. There is another chap in and out of here who went to Brown, too, Maj. Lewis A. Smith '38· Leon Tracy '41 was formerly with us, but has another assignment now. Flemming is adjutant at the headquarters of an airborne training center.

1st Lt. Maxwell G. Hoberman of Robins Field, Ga., says he'd like to hear from Marcus Alper and others. We haven't heard from Alper ourselves since 1942, when he was a Sgt. at Tyndall Field, Panama City, Fla. Hoberman is a graduate of Air Corps Administrative School.

Bob Dugan, with a Railroad Maintenance Unit, expected to draw sergeant stripes when he returned to Louisiana at the end of a two-week leave last month. Hal Carver '30 encountered him in Pennsylvania Station, New York, and reported him in grand condition.

Word reaches us indirectly that Rev. Gardiner H. Shattuck, Chaplain of the Pomfret School since 1942, is returning to Trinity Church, Boston, as assistant minister.

Capt. Earle C. Hochwald makes unnecessary apology for his "abominable typing," explaining that his right hand is in a splint. "I've had many strange and hectic experiences. In March I was wounded in action and am proud of my Purple Heart," the chaplain says. He's been transferred from the medical battalion he was serving in some Pacific jungle and is now with the infantry.

W. O. Jack Roberts has received his

He Jumped on D-Day

▶ RAY HALL '31› the "Parachute Parson," was among the first of the parachute troops to land in Normandy in the morning of the invasion. Henry T. Gorrell, UP correspondent, writing from near Carentan on June 11, said: "I reached this forward observation post in a captured German caterpillar motorcycle under the eyes of German gunners. It was driven by Chaplain Raymond S. Hall, who jumped with the air-borne troops on D-Day and who has been in the front line since, assisting in the handling of heavy casualties under fire."

Later an AP wirephoto showed the former Brown swimmer and the first minister to become a parachute trooper all set, in full regalia, to jump from his plane. ◀

medical discharge from the Army after having been in hospital for 18 months. Jack is now at 1005 West Daniel St., Champaign, Ill., where, we know, he will be happy to hear from any of his friends of college days.

Sgt. H. A. Schulson AAF, is attached to an air squadron at Dodge City, Kan.

Rev. Winthrop M. Mager has left Hurley, N. M., to become assistant pastor of the First Congregational Church, Pasadena, Calif., where his mail address is 464 East Walnut St.

James M. Gicker is Administrative Officer Plant Expansion Section, SC, USA, Philadelphia. Since leaving college Jim has been with American Viscose Corp., Bendix Aviation, Johnson & Johnson, and Sears Roebuck & Co., a varied business and engineering career. His daughter is three years old, and the pride of the Gicker household at 627 Wynnewood Rd., Overbrook, Philadelphia, 31.

Lt. (jg) J. Penn Hargrove, USNR, reports his preferred mail address is 46 Wright St., Westport, Conn. Perhaps when he writes again he'll give us a hint of his naval assignment.

Alfred T. Hill is with Western Electric Co., 120 Broadway, New York, and a resident of Montclair, N. J., with his home at 75 Lloyd Rd.

1934

Pvt. Sumner H. Rogers AAA, is on duty with one of the anti-aircraft batteries training at Ft. Bliss, Tex.

Bob Pottle received commission as Lt. (jg), USNR, at Boston during the spring, we hear. Perhaps Bob or one of his friends on the Hill will see this item, and give us more complete news for the next issue of the ALUMNI MONTHLY.

John M. Sayward's note from Stamford, Conn., is full of news: "Still working for Stamford Labs, American Cyanamid Co.—chemical research. Most of the work is getting more and more tied in with war. Have been out of town most of winter and expect to go again, this time to western Pennsylvania. Am to be married June 29 to Lorraine Anderson, daughter of Mr. and Mrs. William Anderson of Millville, Naugatuck, Conn."

Benjamin D. Crissey is divisional sales manager for Edward Katzinger Co., Chicago, where his office is at 1949 North Cicero Ave. Ed's house and mail address is PO Box 332, Geneva, Ill.

Lt. Dave Caldwell wrote from North Africa that "this duty over here is a great course in 'Appreciation of America.' It's too bad some of those steel and railroad workers can't take it." In three different African ports Dave had encountered Zenas Kevorkian, Lt. Don Ewing '32' and Lt. (jg) Champ Andrews '36' missing Lt. Hank Carpenter by two weeks at one spot. Lt. (jg) Kevorkian came back to the States in May for amphibious training.

Ens. John H. Pennell's letter from New Guinea reached us in May while he and the other Seabees were holding their own in the battle of mud during the rainy season. "We are patiently (?) waiting our next move and some excitement." John was commissioned a year ago in March, fought "the battle of Camp Peary, Williamsburg, Va.," and was assigned to his outfit as Personnel Officer. An interlude at Davisville, R. I., and Christmas in Panama are also part of the record.

Daniel W. Earle, Scout Executive of Seneca Council, Olean, N. Y., was back in

Rhode Island for a brief vacation in May. He was formerly Field Executive of the Narragansett Council.

James M. Libby is an active member of Troop B Cavalry, Connecticut State Guard, the only outfit of its kind in the country. He lives at 810 Farmington Ave., West Hartford. Kenneth T. Piercy was also for long with Troop B as Stable Sgt.—until his firm, General Foods moved him to New York a few months ago. His new address 215 West 98th St. Still another trooper was Frederick H. Rea '35' now a Lt., USAAF, in England, according to Elisha C. Wattles '13' the Captain in command of the Connecticut Cavalry.

1935

Pfc. Henry B. Childs, USMCR, is with the Marines in the SWPA.

Ed Whitehead, Jr., tells us he's been with Carl L. Norden, Inc., makers of the Norden bombsight, for the past year and a half.

Lt. Bill Bigur, Sig C, is in England, according to his younger brother, Art '41'

Campsight in Tokyo?

▶ "WE ARE LOOKING forward to the day when we will drop the ramp on the Island of Japan and set up camp in the centre of Tokyo," writes Lt. Buenos A. W. Young '36' who has seen plenty of action with the Marines. At Eniwetok Atoll he and his battalion made three invasion landings and fought the ensuing battles at Engebi, Eniwetok, and Parry Islands. "Another Brown man I have run across was an engineer in the Class of 1935—Childs (Henry P. Childs, apparently). He is doing a swell job in the communications section of our outfit and went through the above-mentioned invasions landings." ◀

Norman A. Smith is submaster and teacher of history at Thornton Academy, Saco, Me.

1st Lt. Robert L. Eddy's anti-aircraft battalion is now overseas (c/o PM, San Francisco). Dr. Robert D. Eddy, with whom we were not so long ago guilty of confusing him, continues at Tufts as Assistant Professor of Chemistry.

Haven't heard from Eli Levinson since he left for Honolulu. He'd been through the Coast Guard Academy's CRC course and had his commission.

Armand Morin, "who is with Pratt & Whitney, drops in at our base occasionally," according to S/Sgt. Bernard Bell '42' in England.

1936

Lt. (jg) Collamore H. Richmond, USCGR, is aboard a CG cutter in the Pacific area, and is getting his mail through the Fleet PO, San Francisco.

Gordon E. Cadwgan has received his commission as Ensign, USNR, and assigned to Class D-V(S).

1st Lt. James C. Maiden, Jr., AUS, serving as Adjutant, 7th Service Command, Omaha, Neb., was promoted in May.

Capt. Herbert M. Levenson, MC, AUS, is stationed at the Regional Hospital, Sheppard Field, Tex.

Your Secretary records with regret the news that Maj. John J. Zeugner 3rd, AAF, has been killed in action in the North Afri-

A Reject's Record

▶ CAPT. DWIGHT D. PATCH '39' AAF, pilot of a Liberator bomber, has won the DFC. Dwight also holds the Air Medal, which he received for participating in the first flight of bombers raiding the Ploesti oil fields in Romania. He's a veteran of the North African and Sicilian campaigns, having gone over a year ago this summer.

It's worth noting that Dwight made the grade as a pilot after having been rejected by both Army and Navy AC. He enlisted in the Signal Corps, was chief of a ground crew at Pearl Harbor, and then had his chance to go into Air Pilot Training in January, 1943. ◀

can area. Jack, one of our correspondents writes, was CO of his squadron of P-38s and was aboard a transport torpedoed in the Mediterranean. There were no survivors. Jack, recipient of the Air Medal while on submarine patrol duty on this side of the ocean, was a member of the 104th Observation Squadron, Maryland National Guard, when he entered Federal service in February, 1941. To his wife and parents the sympathy of the Class is sincerely given.

Frank Costello is supervisor, Essex Division, Public Service Co-ordinated Transport of New Jersey, with his office at 80 Park Place, Newark, and his home at 1914 Oakwood Parkway, Union, N. J.

Lt. (jg) Stephen N. Burgess USNR, took commission at Boston at the end of May.

Rev. Wesley N. Haines is the new pastor of the First Baptist Church, Freeport, N. Y. As an Ayer Lectureship Foundation Fellow, he's completed his residence work for his Ph.D. at Harvard and intends to write his thesis in absentia. During vacations he has served as councilor and assistant director at Y.M.C.A. camps as training for work among young people.

Ray Parlin is doing development work for Goodyear Fabric Corp. in New Bedford, Mass., where he lives at 74 Jenny Lind St.

Lt. Harry N. Payne, CAC, has recently transferred from Ft. H. G. Wright, N. Y., to the CA Replacement Centre, Ft. Eustis, Va.

Barbara Hanson's note, received June 24, but stamped Feb. 1, says "My husband, John C. Hanson was made Lt. (jg) last month. He has just been home on leave—15 days which flew by in incredibly short order. But they were long enough to enable him to become acquainted with our two-year-old daughter and to win a large spot in her affections."

Lt. Leon M. Payne is in Italy with a bomber group, according to Maj. James L. Whitcomb of Houston, Tex. Jim also gave us a new overseas address for F. J. Watson, BM 2c, USNR, which we're not supposed to publish.

Among the graduates of the Naval War College at its 60th Commencement last month was Lt. (jg) J. Alden Dooley, D-V(S). He took the Preparatory Staff Course at Newport, quite an honor for a jg.

William E. Bright, Jr., was general chairman of the National War Fund campaign last winter which raised Lackawanna County's $232,000 quota in Pennsylvania. His signature was on the special certificates of merit devised for business firms which contributed in recognition of employes with the armed forces. It took a lot of good ideas and hard work to put the drive over, as the *Scranton Tribune* pointed out. Bill is with the Pure Oil Co. in Dickson City.

George H. Ames went through the Aleutian campaign as a 2nd Lt. with the mountain infantry. His brother Knight, a class ahead of us, is a 1st Lt. in the QMC.

1st Lt. Robert Wilkens says he likes his work overseas at a Civil Affairs Center, American School Center. Robert, Jr., is now more than a year old.

Marine Lt. Joe Small went in with the troops that landed at Tarawa, Charlie Drury tells us.

Charlie Kiesel, who went to Hawaii for the Turner Construction Co., is reported transferred to their Chicago district.

Richard M. Rieser used the military form to explain: "1· Unable to comply with basic communication." It had been a letter about the Brown Club meeting in Buffalo in May. The reason was implicit in his military address, for he is a Lt. with a QM Salvage Repair Co. overseas.

1937

Capt. J. D. Crocker is a company commander with a tank destroyer battalion. "MONTHLY sent on to me from home and enjoy following news of Brown and Brown men," he writes.

Bill Watters is the author of "Fighting Sons of the Navy Blue", played coast to coast and overseas by Navy bands and featured widely on the air.· Bill has gone to sea after shore duty with the USN Motion Picture Liaison office in Hollywood. Bill is Y 1/c, USNR, attached to the USNAB, Navy No. 34, with his mail reaching him through the Fleet PO, San Francisco.

Dick Scott is still down in Bluefield, W. Va., with the Esmond Mills. His new house address is Hilltop Lane, Bluefield, Box 316. There's a second daughter, Sarah Chamberlin, in the family now, and Dick has to keep hustling.

Lt. Albion Edgell, USNR, is on board a Navy ship in the Pacific area. In fact, Al is the CO, and we wouldn't mind stepping up on the bridge any day to give him our best First World War salute.

Capt. Ladd McConnell, AAF, came home last month to Laddwood, Matunuck, R. I., after two years of piloting medium bombers and troop transports in the SWPA. He was in the Papuan, New Guinea, and New Britain campaigns. "Only routine," he told a *Providence Journal* interviewer; nevertheless he had several warm experiences on bombing missions against

Jap airfields, harbors, and shipping. As a boy, he had malaria in Africa, and escaped it in the South Pacific.

A recent issue of the *Providence Sunday Journal* carried an excellent picture of Pvt. Alan V. Young, USA, Mrs. Young, and their son, Curtis Gidley Young, who should be ready for Brown in 1961 or 1962. We saw Alan in Providence early in the spring. He came home from the West Coast because of the serious illness of his father.

Fred Sawyer is a mechanical engineer with Stone & Webster Engineering Corp.· and is working at the Butyl Rubber Plant of the corporation in Baytown, Tex.

Lt. Leon F. Eisman, USNR, recently went over to the Marine Division, his mother reports from Charleston, W. Va., and reported for temporary duty at the Marine Base, San-Diego, Calif. ·

T/4 James R. Rigby, Inf., is in training with a division at Camp Claiborne, La. Jim is with the construction company of his regiment, if our guess that Cn Co. means that unit of heavy duty workers and fighters, too.

While stationed at NTS, Farragut, Idaho, Harvey R. Nanes' commission caught up with him last April and he went to the University of Arizona for indoctrination, which he finished June 12. He's been ordered to Ft. Schuyler for further training.

Donald Stewart has been for some time an associate editor of *Fortune* magazine, in New York. Previously he edited College Texts for Scott, Foresman of Chicago.

Dr. Harold S. Barrett, in the U. S. Public Health Service with the rank of Assistant Surgeon, has been appointed Director of the Yazoo County Health Department, and Mrs. Barrett has joined him to live at 227 North Main St., Yazoo City, Miss. He's also on the staff of the King's Daughters' Hospital. He went there from Washington where he was working in the Division of States Relations of the U. S. P. H. S.

Lt. (jg) Allyn Brown, Jr., USCGR, is aboard a DE in the Atlantic.

Evan M. Crossley, S2c, was transferred to the Recreation Department of the Seabees this spring and is in charge of one of the libraries at Camp Peary, Va.

1938

Dr. Chauncey M. Stone, Jr., brings us to date with this welcome paragraph: "Entered Army Jan. 2, 1944, after 10 months' internship at Boston City Hospital. Went to Camp Barkley, Abilene, Tex., for preliminary training and from there was sent to William Beaumont General Hospital,

El Paso. Living in El Paso for past three months with wife, Muriel Baker Stone '37· Pembroke College."

Lt. (jg) Henry J. Rohrs, Ch C, USNR, reports his address is 3029 South Columbus St.; Arlington, Va.

Lt. (jg) Leo Loeb, Jr., USNR, is back in the States again after nine months as skipper of an LCT in the SWPA.' He's now at the USNATB Solomons, Md., as an instructor in the LCT training program. "Surely is wonderful to be back," he wrote. "One of my Christmas presents was Dr. Wriston's new book, 'Challenge to Freedom,' which I am enjoying to the full. Also continue to enjoy my copies of the ALUMNI MONTHLY, and am especially pleased to note the large Navy training program in effect on the campus."

Lt. Col. Raymond Renola, USA, who left us to accept appointment to West Point, where he shone as a baseball player, was home on leave last month. He's CO of the 375th Fa Bn, 100th Infantry Division, Ft. Bragg, N. C. Renola was graduated from West Point in 1940.

Ens. Arthur H. Noble, Jr., is on duty at the ATB Ft. Pierce, Fla., to which he went from the Amphibious Base at Little Creek, Va.

Capt. J. J. Muller has a new assignment. Previous to May 1 he had been with headquarters at the 11th Port of Embarkation in England, aide to the General in command. He found port work interesting and varied, with all its ramifications and problems. Now he's in a related business at an Advance Section Communication Zone headquarters. One of the few who has encountered no fellow Brunonians, he writes in appreciation of the news letters and the ALUMNI MONTHLY, which "keeps us in touch with everyone—at least from an academic and detached point of view."

Lt. (jg) C. Hudson Thompson, Jr., reports a brief chat with Phil Glatfelder overseas "aboard a warship." While in New York following the sinking of the Beatty, his ship, Hudson saw Harrie Hart '36 a number of times at 90 Church St., where Harrie is Personnel Officer.

News comes roundabout that Bob Brush has his Army commission and is in California.

Lt. Arthur Newell, Jr., is at the Naval Liaison office in Port Said where his knowledge of the Eastern languages is put to good use.

2nd Lt. Roland A. Hueston, Jr., overseas with a weather squadron "somewhere out of San Francisco," writes in appreciation of news from the campus. "I met a classmate on the way 'over, Pvt. Sherwood C. Haskins and had several long talks with him."

Lt. Bill Wolfe "finally made it overseas," he told us in June. "For the time being I'm in Australia and soon will move to greener fields and see lots." He wants his magazine to follow him.

Lt. Jim Gurll, too, continues as an Australian and reports a recent reunion with Lt. (jg) Jim Brown '36 and Capt. Karl Morton '40· the latter with six months' duty previously in Iceland. Morton is a new, proud father. Gurll wanted the address of Karl Patterson, his old roommate, so that he could congratulate him on being a father again, too. Recovering from a broken hand, Gurll was on temporary duty in the ordnance section of his fleet's Commander Service Force, but hoped to be back in the States later this summer.

46

Report from India, a Way Station

▶ ▶ SGT. A. S. NANES '41' whose outfit has been bombing Japan of late, writes: "Knowing that Brown men can be found anywhere and everywhere in this man's army, I did a little scouting around my own group and found Sal Virgadamo '36' working in the intelligence section. The conversation soon took on the familiar aspects of old home week. What with Al Barber '44 also present, the nucleus is there for the first Brown Club of India. (Sorry, Al, but the Brunonians with the Rhode Island Hospital medical unit have already the claim on that distinction for a year.)

"I've a piece of news about my outfit, by the way. They're the boys who just bombed Japan in the new B-29's. Having been with this project virtually since its inception, you get a thrill to see· all the plans and training bear some fruit. Everyone feels that his efforts deserve a small scale pat on the back, and that we have received.

"No need to repeat how welcome the MONTHLY is. It keeps my memories of college fresh and evergreen. Well, here's hoping that soon we're all gathered at that big post-war reunion." ◀ ◀

Roger Francis, T/5, writes to Andy Comstock '10 that he is now "chaplain's assistant, with a new unit, activated only a month ago."

1939

Capt. David Landman, Inf., who has moved pretty much over the country in the course of training, is getting his mail nowadays through APO 93, c/o Postmaster, San Francisco.

Capt. Thomas C. Roberts, FA, recently transferred from Ft. Sill, Okla., to Camp Chaffee, Ark.

Lt. John T. Barrett, MC, AUS, reports his current address is MDRP, Stark General Hospital, Charleston, S. C.

Lyman G. Friedman is a lawyer with Stinson, Mag, Thomson, McEvers & Fizzell, with his office at 201 First National Bank Rd., and his home at 3509 Gillham Rd., Kansas City, Mo.

We've recently seen a fine picture of George Truman, who won his wings and commission as Ensign, USNR, at the NATC, Corpus Christi, Tex., in May.

From Burma last month came four 10 rupee notes, a total of 40 rupees drawn on the Reserve Bank of India and guaranteed by the Central Government. The sender was Lt. G. Holmes Wilson, our champion diver, and the money was for the E. Leo Barry Memorial Fund. "Coach Barry was much more to me than a coach, as I had known him ever since I was big enough to make a splash off a springboard," Holmes wrote. "Any success I had as a diver at Brown, I owe in large measure to his help and guidance. . . . Heartiest congratulations to this year's team. It surely did a grand job." Holmes said that although he was deep in "the lousiest jungle" he ever hoped to see, "mail does actually find me in time, and I'm always glad to get it even if most of the news is history by the time it arrives."

Dud Zinke, who has an honorable medical discharge from the Navy, is a flight navigator for United Air Lines "flying the Pacific as contract carriers for the ATC, AAF." In a letter last month he wrote: "To date I have flown about 15 round trips to Australia and have visited most of the island groups in the Pacific now held by our forces." Dud lives at 425 San Mateo Drive, San Mateo, Calif.

S/Sgt. John Leland writes (c/o PM, San Francisco): "We have moved again and are in the usual stage of discomfort attendant on a change of location and the building of a new camp. We don't much care where we go, but we do hate the transition and would just as soon limit ourselves to one more year. Unfortunately,

the Army has other plans for us. . . . The first group of men to be returned to the States left the squadron a week ago, so the 'going-home bill' is now something more than a fairy-tale to be read in the papers and magazines. Everyone was so happy about it that there weren't any false rumors spread for nearly a week; no one talked of anything else."

Samuel N. Bogorad of the Department of English at Northwestern reports: "I had a painful awareness of how old I'm getting when recently one of my students in English (Freshman) had a date with an officer-candidate in our Abbott Hall, and he turned out to be David Marshall, a student in the first class I taught at Brown in 1940!"

"Charlie Gustaveson, the high jumper, walked into the BOQ here yesterday," wrote Lt. (jg) Ed Armstrong '42' USCGR, from the Key West Fleet Sound School. "He's on a 'can' and is a Navy Ensign."

Rev. Walter N. Jackson has been serving this past year as Protestant minister in a large housing project of war workers' families, Herman Gardens Housing Project at Detroit (8641 Grandmont). The Sunday after D-Day he preached the following theme: "This is not God's war. The Allies are not launched on any Christian crusade. All the nations are involved in an unholy mess. God's judgment is upon all of the nations for past stupidities and sins." Jackson writes: "Strangely enough, this sermon to war workers and their wives was more enthusiastically received than any I have yet preached."

1st Lt. Joe Blessing paid his respect to the Deans and the Alumni Office this month, home on furlough. He looked well and was just starting to relax after 53 bombing missions in the New Guinea area. The Army promoted him in April.

2nd Lt. Robert F. Garner is an addition to our military roster. He's been with the headquarters battery of a Coast Artillery outfit in the Pacific. Harold E. Miller '07 tells us that Mrs. Garner and the child are living in New Brunswick.

1st Lt. Ed Brown is overseas with a cavalry reconnaissance squadron, his father writes from Cleveland.

2nd Lt. William M. Canby, CAC, wrote from Ft. Fisher, N. C., that he'd moved so frequently of late he had hard work keeping us posted of his address. He's with a Corps Hq Det.

Frank Comstock was home on furlough recently while the mine sweeper of which he is skipper was being overhauled.

T/Sgt. Robert D. O'Brien writes that Mrs. O'Brien and he are living on the Post at Fort Monroe (15 Murray Rd.) where he is instructing in the Master Gunner School in the Coast Artillery School. "We will welcome any Brown men—Army or Navy—who hit this spot. And many do. Last one we saw was Ens. Wally Lineburgh '38' just prior to his receiving a new assignment."

1940

1st Lt. John J. McLaughry, USMCR, with Carlson's Raiders until the unit was made a part of the 4th Marine Regiment, has had malaria and jaundice out there in the SWPA, but is back in action once more. His promotion came through in May.

Bruce Robbins has completed his test course at the River Works, General Electric Co., Lynn, Mass., and is working as a project engineer in the Turbosupercharger Engineering Division. "I've been married since last August to Aubrey Pope of St. Louis, Mo.," he reports from 17 Beach Rd., Lynn.

Lt. Raymond F. Curran, USNR, is aboard one of the well known Navy destroyers, on active duty in Atlantic waters.

Cliff Lathrop has moved from Jacksonville to Glenarm, Md., where he is a planning engineer with Glen L. Martin Co. "Bumped into Lt. Luke Mayer '38, USNR, who is stationed at the Bethlehem Shipyards," he noted on his postcard.

Ken Heinold is in the Navy, and Bob Mignone is in the Army, we hear, but we have no direct word as to their respective ranks and stations.

Harvey W. Dennis, Jr., is an accountant with Pittsburgh Plate Glass Co., Providence and lives at 192 Anthony St., East Providence.

Bill McCullough has received commission as Ensign, with assignment to SC-V(P).

Brown Alumni Monthly

Published at Brown University by the Associated Alumni

CHESLEY WORTHINGTON '23
Managing Editor

ARTHUR BRAITSCH '23
Business Manager

HENRY S. CHAFEE '09
LOUIS B. PALMER '28' LT. (jg), USNR
ALFRED H. GURNEY '07
GERTRUDE ALLEN MacCONNELL '10
Pembroke Correspondent

Subscriptions, $2 a year. Single copies, 25 cents. There is no issue during August or September.

Entered at the Providence Post Office as second-class matter.

| Vol. XLV | SUMMER, 1944 | No. 2 |

Lt. Frank S. Williams, Jr., AAF, back from 10 months of flying and fighting in southern and eastern Europe, "has declared a personal war on Rhode Island lobsters," said an illustrated story in the *Providence Evening Bulletin*, June 16. And there was Frank's picture with a big lobster on the table, all ready for demolishing. "He had a cold boiled lobster before he went to bed last night," the story went on. "He had lobster for lunch today. He said he intends to have broiled lobster for dinner tonight." Pork chops came next after lobster. Between meals, Frank admitted to having been on 50 missions, some of them "pretty rough," and to having had the daylights scared out of him the first time he saw rockets from the German-rocket launching planes. He took a crack at the Romanian oil fields, bombed targets in Austria, and hit Munich and other enemy centres. He wears the Air Medal with six Oak Leaf Clusters. After his 21-day leave, he reported to Atlantic City for rest and then for re-assignment.

Ray Comyn is an Ensign in the USNR, with his home and present mail address, 3 Banham Ave., Quaker Hill, Conn.

Duncan W. Cleaves is still with the Chile Exploration Co. at Chuquicamata, Chile, working at the mine there which is probably the largest single copper-ore body in the world and one of the largest copper producers. The mining town is 10,000 feet high in the north Chilean Stacama Desert near the nitrate fields of Marie Elena and at the edge of the Andes. A few months before the United States entered the war, Duncan signed a three-year contract as chemical engineer with the Chile Exploration Co., a subsidiary of Anaconda. In Chuquicamata he met and married Sara Lazarte Vince on June 6, 1942.

Since Peter DeNyse Brown, born Feb. 12 to Ens. and Mrs. Frederick D. Brown, has had a total of eight forebears at Brown, the father hopes "we'll see him at Brown in the Class of '66'" Fred was at the Navy's Diesel Engineering School at Cornell when he wrote but by now may be seeing sea duty.

Take it for what it's worth: Lt. William Reisman, invited in one of our recent mailings to "use space below for news item about yourself," wrote in: "Boo! Wounded in action in Tennessee. Escaped from a death worse than fate."

"There must be a lot of us here now, caulking our boats to cross the Channel," Charley Vivian wrote from England before the invasion, "but I have only run across Steve Stephanos '41 and Capt. Bob Poole '40' the latter a meteorological expert in the

Air Corps. Myself, I just keep watching those caissons go rolling along." (As a Captain.)

Writing last month from SMAAF, San Marcos, Tex., 2nd Lt. Harold W. Pfautz reported the following there at navigation school: Lt. R. Clifford, Lt. S. Jagolinzer, and Lt. B. Lurbarsky '43.

Lt. Irving Twomey, meteorologist with the Army Air Corps somewhere in Greenland, writes that the mountain heights and glacial formations are breathtaking in their beauty; that the land is lonesome but dramatic. One pleasant encounter was with Major Bob Sykes '39' who is "in charge of weather in that region." Irving wants his magazine sent direct to him, rather than to his home in Newport.

Last January Lt. (jg) Walter R. Hall told us he was on the Transport Susan B. Anthony. Since that was one of the ships sunk on D-Day, we're hoping to hear of his news and new billet.

1941

Capt. John A. Kidney, USMCR, home last month from the SWPA, was a campus visitor, with the news that he had seen Lt. Bill Paine, who is flying Corsairs; Lt. Don McNeil '40' CO of a fighter unit; Lt. Harry Whynaught '42' who is also flying Corsairs; and Lt. John J. McLaughry '40' Jack was looking so well that we spoke of the fact. He laughed, and said he had put on 20 pounds since landing in this country. We've reported previously on Jack's dive bombing over Kolombangara and elsewhere.

Lt. Theodore A. Kagels, Jr., AAF, who was an A/C last time we heard from him, is getting his mail in care of his mother, Mrs. T. A. Kagels, Dale Rd., Newfane, N. Y.

S/Sgt. Robert S. Cohn's latest address, he reports, is 158th Liaison Sqdn, RDAAF, Raleigh, N. C.

When he sent in his subscription to the ALUMNI MONTHLY last month, Lt. John K. Ellenbogen, told us his current address is Navy 122, Box 11, c/o Fleet PO, New York, N. Y.

T/5 Merwin F. Bailey, USA, has written his parents, Mr. and Mrs. Sidney Bailey of East Haven, Conn., that he has arrived in the SWPA. He's with a chemical unit, with which he trained in Maryland, Alabama, and California.

Dick Baumann, recently given his honorable discharge from the Army, is in the furniture business with D. Baumann & Co., Inc., 2922 Third Ave., The Bronx, N. Y.

Rev. Alvin Holt Hanson is curate of Grace Cathedral, Topeka, Kan., where he and Mrs. Hanson, the former Roberta Beatrice Tripp, live at 1241 College Ave. While Al was at the Episcopal Theological School, Cambridge, he was assistant to the Chaplain at the Massachusetts State Prison, Charlestown.

Pete Laudati, Lt., AAF, who was in the thick of it in the Mediterranean area as a weather officer, came home on leave last month. He's been away two years. "Even the sight of a field of corn thrilled him," said "Army" Armstrong '42' who rode with Pete on the train home from Florida. Well, according to all reports, Pete had a memorable homecoming, saw most of his friends, the races, and made the most of his days off duty before reporting to his next assignment.

"Army," who also ran into Lt. Arthur W. Smith, USNR, wrote: "He's a quiet fellow

but full of fun. A year and a half of giving the yellow boys hell from a dive bomber hasn't changed him a bit." Pete is getting a new assignment.

Lt. Norman S. Dike, Jr., parachutist, was under final orders the last week in May, his father, Judge Norman S. Dike '85' wrote.

Capt. Art Bijur, Sig C, (note the promotion) writes from somewhere under the British influence at the Pacific end of the world to say that he had gained 2 stones 2 since he'd been "in this beautiful country," and feels fine again. He compares notes by V-mail with Giles MacEwan, a Lt. in the Air Corps in Italy, and has heard that Lou Duesing, also an Air Corps Lt., is back in the States "after doing Africa."

John Mars, with a medical discharge from the Army, hopes to complete his work in Harvard graduate school by the end of the summer. He's living at home: 152 Blue Hill Ave., Milton.

George Gibbons' five-year-old New England Intercollegiate record in the 300-yard individual medley swim was broken this spring when another Brown captain, Carl Paulson, sliced 4½ seconds off Gibby's time of 3:40.5.

Pfc. C. Shaw Murray expects to finish medical school this September. On a recent visit to the Alumni Office he said Lt. John James had finished training his outfit at Ft. Monmouth.

Arthur J. Vierling, weather officer in an AAF B-17 Flying Fortress Group operating from an Italian base in the 15th Air Force, has been promoted to the rank of 1st Lt. His job consists of charting and handling weather observations. Overseas for three months, his organization was recently commended by the Commanding General of the 15th Air Force for its performance. Lt. Vierling was with the Remington Arms Company in Bridgeport, Conn., at the time of his induction in 1942. He attended the Army Weather School at M. I. T.

With the Yanks in Russia

▶ ▶ "I'M FINALLY allowed to tell you where I am," 1st Lt. C. Harrison Meyer '41 wrote on June 9. "I'm in the first American outfit to fight in Russia. Don't believe there are any other Brown men here, but I wouldn't trade my experiences with anyone's. Wish I could tell you how I got here and a lot of other things, but I've told all I can for the time being until they tell us officially what we can and cannot say."

Meyer's V-mail letter solves the mystery in his previous note, received last April: "Have left jolly ol' England and am now headed for a distant destination where I don't expect to run into any Brown men."

On July 1 he wrote again: "Had a Cook's tour of half the world getting here, traveling the hard way. The Russian people are very friendly toward us, and we're picking up their language fairly rapidly. We've had our share of excitement already, but I'm none the worse off from it. Just received and finished reading the Jan.-Feb. issue of the MONTHLY, and sure enjoyed it." ◀ ◀

Jewett's Favorite Story

▶ LT. WILLIAM A. JEWETT '41' USNR, is CO of a converted minesweeper, one of the few vessels with Navy personnel operating in the Greenland Patrol. Martin Sheridan, former Providence newspaperman and now a free lance war correspondent, had chow with Bill not long ago, and wrote about it for the *Providence Sunday Journal*.

"Jewett's favorite story concerns a British mine that floated ashore in Greenland and was taken apart by Eskimos, who carried off samples of TNT for souvenirs. Jewett was visiting a Danish administrator a year after the incident occurred when he noticed a polished detonator atop a stack of papers on the man's desk." Neither could understand the other; so Jewett took the detonator, connected it with batteries, threw it overboard, and pressed the button after getting into a safe position. The explosion "all but floored the Dane. He turned as white as a hospital wall, sagged a bit, and wiped his damp forehead, while muttering something in Danish that must have meant, 'Man, what a close call!'"

Bob Braithwaite was married last fall while a Pfc. at Carleton College's ASTU in Minnesota. His wife was a senior working for a Music degree at St. Olaf College there at Northfield.

Ens. N. C. de Paul, Jr., SC, USNR, "having finally come to rest in one corner of the globe in a more or less permanent billet," sends us his address: NOB, Navy 153, FPO, N. Y.

Capt. Stephen G. Stone Jr., who deals in bombing from England, says he saw Frank Drummond '42 about six weeks ago (that would have been in May). "He is M/Sgt. in charge of the Intelligence Section of a Bomb Group."

Steve reports Walt Commander '42 somewhere in Italy, a Field Artillery officer. "Then last week I heard from Chan Murray '41' who is up at Tufts Medical School, and the same day the April ALUMNI MONTHLY arrived, so I'm pretty well up to date on what's going on around Providence."

1st Lt. Rodman S. Moeller of the antiaircraft remarks that sending us a change of address seems to be a weekly occurrence. Thinks we'll "soon need a special file clerk to keep track of one Lt." Rod says he "met one Brown grad at POE, fellow with glasses, about class '40' who worked in the John Hay." Well, that narrows the field slightly.

Lt. Lewis I. Schwartz, late of the Technical Data Lab at Wright Field, is now at the Contract Termination School at the Dayton Army Air Field in Vandalia, O.

Aboard a mine-sweeper in the South Pacific, Bob Keedick reports: "It's not such a bad location at present, and I've had the good luck to run into Foster B. Davis '39 and Larry Hall '42 lately. I always keep my eye peeled for Brown men. It sure is a treat to receive the MONTHLY even though they are usually several months old before their arrival."

Ens. Everett J. Daniels bumped into Lt. (jg) Skip Stahley several times while they were at Ft. Schuyler NTS together. His meeting with Lt. Carl Bridenbaugh was a daily occurrence, for his old Brown prof was his instructor in Fundamentals. Among Brown men encountered in New York were Lt. (jg) Ronnie McIntyre, USCGR, and Reeven Novogrod '38' War Department field representative.

William H. Collins, Jr., is now a Lt., USNR, on a destroyer escort in the North Atlantic. He saw Vic Schwartz '40 in Brazil last year and Dick Wilbur in Guantanamo Bay, Cuba, shortly after. "Otherwise, few Brown men have crossed my path."

Lt. Bob Rapelye, in England with a photo reconaissance squadron, spotted Arthur

Brown's name in a Red Cross book. He reports Cpl. Charles Hammett '42 overseas in the Pacific.

Stuart Whipple, son of C. M. Whipple '09 is a Captain on the Burma India front. On his first assignment, four enlisted men and he won an Air Force Citation—the Air Combat Star. Twin boys, Stuart, Jr., and Steven, have been born since he went overseas. Stu was the first volunteer under the Selective Service Act in his district in Washington, D. C., in October, 1940.

2nd Lt. Theodore A. Kagels, Jr., went to Roswell, N. M. for further training after graduation from the AAF Navigation School at Monroe, La.

Lt. (jg) H. N. Volk recently returned after 14 months in the Sopac during which time he saw Major R. W. Kenny of the English Dept., Capt. Art Bijur, Lt. J. K. Solfisburg, USNR '41' Lt. (jg) E. J. Cronin '39' Lt. (jg) Woods '40' (Thomas B. Wood '39?). At the Amphibious Training Base in Virginia last month, he reported other Brunonians there: Ens. H. D. Sharpe, Jr., '45' Lt. (jg) Leon Rogers '40' and Lt. Moore, USNR '41' (?). Lt. (jg) H. Eliot Rice '41 of the LST staff, Solomons, Md., was a recent visitor.

From Douglas Gutenkunst's commander and through the courtesy of his family we learn the details of his death last winter: "We were coming in to land after dark, after an attack on Japanese shipping, and as he swung in to land, another plane, whose pilot had been apparently shot up by Japanese fighters, collided with him in mid-air killing them both instantly. Doug was recovered from the wreckage and, after positive identifications by our doctor, was buried in a simple, impressive military funeral conducted by a Catholic Navy Chaplain at Army Cemetery, Number One, Torokine, Bougainville Island.

"Doug had flown brilliantly as my wing man for many months, and we had become very close friends. His cheerful ways and quick mind made him a valued member of the Squadron. . . . On the 26th of January we had gone together, as always, on an attack of a Japanese stronghold and to my (and his) delight he shot down four Jap planes for sure. For this action, which gave him a chance to show what an expert pilot he really was, he will be recommended for decoration. On the afternoon of the 30th, we had a hurry-up call for fighters, and Douglas volunteered to go with me to help foray the escort for the bombers, although he had already completed one dangerous mission that day. We were safely home and all but ready for supper when the tragedy struck."

1942

Rev. H. Russell Barker is assistant at the Chapel of the Incarnation (Episcopal) 240 East 31st St., New York.

A/C Alfred T. Marshall is in training, we hear, down in San Marcos, Tex.

Pvt. Henry J. Hoye, Jr., Inf., is learning how to be a foot soldier with a division currently going through its paces at Camp Van Dorn, Miss.

Lt. E. Falcon John, AAF, is a prisoner of war held by the Germans. His father, Lt. Col. Ernest John, Inf. USA has sent us the news adding that Falcon has been in German hands since the last week in April.

Ens. Charles E. Spencer, 3rd, USNR, gives his new mail address, 189 Temple St. West Newton, Mass. Charlie who was Assistant Personnel Manager, Electric Boat Co., Groton, Conn., before entering service was married in May as you may have already heard. His wife is the former Catherine Elizabeth Ahern.

"Orders to report to Ft. Benning, Ga., rescinded. Address all correspondence to me at Ft. Jackson, S. C.," Herb Katz wrote late in May.

Ens. Edmund F. Armstrong, USCGR, is doing sea duty on a cutter based near New York. "We have a ball team on here now that I sort of play guardian angel to—and first base for," he said in a recent letter to his Providence newspaper friend, Jack Martin. "Haven't been organized long, and we are a little short on practice. But we have some pretty hot players." Coming home from Sound School at Key West not long ago, "Army" met Lt. Pete Laudati '41' just back from two years overseas, and he and Pete had a grand time swapping stories.

Davol H. Meader, FD, USA, has been promoted to 1st Lt. That FD unless we are mistaken, stands for Finance Department, a logical place for Davol, as his father, W. Granville Meader '05 is one of Rhode Island's best known bankers.

Jack Ashworth is a chemist in the Department of Physical Chemistry, Harvard Medical School.

John M. Hoffman, Jr., reports a change of address to 232 East King St., Chambersburg, Pa.

Terry Thompson wrote Andrew B. Comstock '10 that he is in Italy. In August last he ran into Bob Fallon in Algiers and Lou Duesing in Oran.

Pfc. Charles A. Leach, Jr., continues at Harvard Medical School under the ASTP set-up. His address: 250 Vanderbilt Hall, Boston 15.

Lt. James T. Sloan, Jr., sent us an Australian pound in payment of his ALUMNI MONTHLY, which follows him overseas to his QM job at Division Headquarters.

Cpl. Richard Hulme has been in Italy but was in Africa when he sent a new address in June for his magazine mailing.

Lt. Charles T. Lloyd, with the infantry at Camp Butner, N. C., liked our picture and story on Sapinsley and Dolley in Sicily. "That street photographer ought to be on someone's staff," he thought. He sent us the clipping about Adolph Wochomurka, used elsewhere.

Joe Weisberger is still up in New Guinea, or was when Jim Gurll '38 wrote us just before Commencement.

As an old Sock and Buskin stalwart, Frank Drummond got a big kick when he had a pass for a London opening night recently and found Royalty also on hand.

When 1st Lt. William L. Irvine, Jr., wrote us, he was still in the Hammond General Hospital, Modesto, Cal. He had been a company officer in an infantry rifle regiment at Pearl Harbor time, was executive officer in a machine gun company while at the time he was injured overseas in December, 1942.

From S/Sgt. Bernard Bell in England: "Since I've been over here I've bumped into Lt. (jg) Ken Clapp '40' S/Sgt. George Hurley '41' Cpl. Howard Arnold '42' and Lt. Gene Coughlin '42' who just came over. I'm sweating out OCS and hoping to be back for our fifth reunion." We sent him the names of Maj. Dave McGovern and Sgt. Thomas J. Hunt, Jr., listed on the Stars and Stripes register as at the same APO number.

1st Lt. Ed MacGowan of the Marines has been awarded a silver star, under what circumstances we hope to learn.

Lt. (jg) Joseph F. Lockett, Jr., likes the sea and his work as assistant communications officer aboard an escort carrier, his father tells us.

Lt. (jg) Jack Sullivan has been instructing at Lauderdale Beach Hotel, Ft. Lauderdale since last summer, following special training at the Washington Navy Yard.

Lt. E. Biddle Conklin, Jr., Sig. C. has been in England for some time and has done quite a bit of work with the British troops.

1943

One of our best correspondents — and fortunately we have many — is Lt. Joseph E. Cook, Jr., of Chanute Field. (He and his bride, the former Ellen Pine '45' are living in Champaign.) He graduated from the AAFTS at Yale March 2 after 18 weeks' prepping at Yale as a communications officer, then had orientation at AACS, Ft. Knox. Chanute is his seventh station in a year, as we figure it. Along the way he picked up a lot of Brown news: from Pfc. J. R. Roan at McClellan Field, Cal., Pfc. W. P. Saunders with Hq. Det. at Camp Beale, Cal.; D. F. Finn with the infantry at Ft. Jackson, S. C.; Pfc. E. H. Dahlquist at Tufts Medical; Cpl. M. F. Stockwell in England; Lt. W. S. Prebluda and Lt. R. C. Houck in an AACS training unit at Godman Field, Ky.; Lt. J. H. Alger of Bradley Field's weather detachment in Connecticut; A/C W. W. Keffer at Yale. "I'm plugging Brown wherever I go and have more or less acquired the name of Joe E. Brown now instead of my own. . . . I get your magazine regularly and don't miss a word of it."

Lester Vargas led his class at George Washington Medical School under the ASTP and made, we're told, the second highest grade ever awarded in the National Board exams. He hopes to be at Rhode Island Hospital in February to start his interning.

Bruce M. Donaldson, supervisor of training for Pusey and Jones Corp. in Wilmington, Del., has a new address. He and his bride are living at Meadow Woods, Bellevue.

Ens. Bill Sullivan was assigned to a destroyer on graduation from Columbia Midshipman's School.

When the father and mother of Jim Rutherford visited the Alumni Office recently, they had heard of the circumstances of his death. His plane was one of a flight of seven returning from a mission over

---

Munda. Running into a sudden storm, only two planes were able to avoid it; the others vanished into it, including Jim's. Jim's record had been of the best. He'd been fifth in his class and had been sent overseas after only 40 hours' flying time. The Rutherfords have been told that an Air Medal is on the way.

2nd Lt. Dwight Ladd, USMCR, left Johnny Truelson in California when he came east to join a 75mm howitzer battalion, which "promises" to be the best in a long line of "best" Marine outfits. He called his gift to the Alumni Fund "a sort of last act before leaving to join the other Brunonians out Tojo-way."

A/C Henry Austin, USNR, was in the Alumni Office recently before going on to Pre-flight School. He was on indefinite leave because weather conditions had held up the class ahead of him.

Stephen Ring, now a Captain in the USAAC, was commended with his crew last November for sinking one Japanese destroyer and badly damaging another.

Lt. Phil Carson's wife has arrived safely in Great Britain for work with the Red Cross.

Ens. Charles P. Littlefield is skipper of an LCT in the ETO. So far the only Brown man he's run into is Richard Palmer '43 who's attached to amphibious small boats.

Frederick Mason, Jr., BM 1c USCGR, was in the thick of things during invasion operations off Normandy.

Lt. Jack Andrews, USMCR, writes that he is "just an A.E.F. (American exiled in Florida) stuck in a camp in Florida studying something entirely over my head." (We don't believe that last part.)

Sgt. Jack Hess has made several crossings of the Atlantic with the Army's transport service, to which he is assigned.

"It seems this sort of stuff will go on for the duration," 1st Lt. Rodman S. Moeller V-mailed giving a new address overseas (c/o Postmaster, N. Y.) He's in anti-aircraft.

Robert D. Schmalz received his silver wings and commission as 2nd Lt. at Spence Field, Moultrie, Ga., May 23. His bride (see Weddings) is an alumna of Wheaton College, lately on the laboratory staff at Boston's Faulkner Hospital.

"A recent meeting of a Brown Club in the Pacific Isles" was the caption of a snapshot sent us last month by Robert Rulon Miller of Waynesboro, Va. The photograph had been sent to his wife and showed her brother Ed Leahy '41' Harvey Spear '22' Ed Cunningham '41' Dave Cooper '43' and Eliot Miller '43' It was a good picture, but we thought, inasmuch as Spear, Cooper, and Miller were on a recent cover they might feel themselves overpublicized.

Ens. Con Prudden is commanding an LCT in the Pacific.

We caught up with Cpl. Howard Braverman just in time: "I was quite happy to have received my first copies of the magazine shortly before I left Africa for this theatre. Believe me when I say that I spent several really enjoyable hours reading them over and I felt once again close to many of those whom I hold to be very dear friends. At my present station I have once again seen an old friend of mine and one of the school's—Art Brown '41'"

Bob McGowan, reported missing since his April bombing raid over Ploesti, Romania, was listed July 14 officially as killed in action.

Don Corzine, Navy flier, received his commission in May. "Airplane jockey," he called himself. A later letter from Dwight Ladd said Don was still in flight training at Melbourne, Fla.

1944

S/Sgt. George Campbell, Jr., has a fine commendation in his 201 file, thanks to his commanding officer at the Basic Training Centre, Greensboro, N. C. The latter, 1st Lt. Robert Campbell, Jr. (no relation), had been praised for the training of the group under his command and proceeded to share the credit. Sgt. Campbell's father, a member of the class of 1907, told of the honor at the recent meeting of the Brown alumni in Buffalo. His address: 909 Genesee Building, Buffalo 2.

John Buchman was promoted to Lt. (jg) in the USNR the first of May. He was in the first group of NROTC men to be commissioned at Brown last June.

Ens. Christy Karafotias has now changed his name legally to Christy Karr.

Chandler Swallow, Jr., who attended Brown for a year before going on to Annapolis, received his Ensign's commission this June.

Pvt. Leslie B. Cohen, with a troop carrier squadron (c/o PM, Seattle), has run into Brown men all over the country. One was Roy Swingler at Drew Field in December.

2nd Lt. Frederick C. Williams Jr., USAAC, stopped in at the Alumni Office on his way to his new post in Ohio where he is going to learn to fly "four-engined boxcars," B-17's in other words. He received his wings at Seymour, Ind., in May.

Donald R. Parker, who had been in the Naval Reserve, Class V-7, for more than a year prior to commencement, reported on Oct. 29, 1943, to the New York Midshipman's School, as an engineering officer candidate. He received his Ensign's Commission on Feb. 24, 1944, at impressive ceremonies in the Cathedral of St. John the Divine in N. Y. On Mar. 16, Donald reported to the Naval Training School, Diesel Engine Division at Pennsylvania State College for a four months' course. Notice of his marriage appears elsewhere.

Pfc. Irving R. Levine, now in the Signal Corps at Camp Crowder, says he hated to leave Denver, where he was in the Denver U's ASTP unit. He speaks with gratitude of the hospitality shown the three Brown men in it by Judge Joseph E. Cook '14' He doesn't say who they were, but Frank Graves '45' John Cuccolo '46' Francis Cole '43' and Stewart Sweet '44 had been among the electrical engineers assigned to D. U. for training.

Lt. H. Hector Rafuse, USAAC navigator, was injured in an aircraft accident somewhere overseas last winter. He's written from Morocco to tell of having joined the Short Snorters.

Pfc. Tim Joyner, transferred to Quantico this spring reports that the following classmates were with him at Parris Island: Jasper Olmstead, John Ross, Peter Pearson, Arthur Marx, Herbert Sherman, Robert Klie, Bradford Whitman, William Reid (all in the same platoon) and John Baer. The ALUMNI MONTHLY, sent him by another alumnus, was passed around among them all—"to their infinite delight."

Three Ensigns, aboard the same new heavy cruiser since graduation in October, 1943,—D. A. E. Wood, W. H. Kimball and W. E. Jessup, Jr. Jessup wrote the ALUMNI MONTHLY on June 26: "Recently our ship has done some plain and fancy shooting in the invasion of the Baie de la Seine. P. S. They shot back with enough accuracy to jangle all our nerves."

Pfc. Jack Conklin is taking the medical course at Columbia and living in Bard Hall.

Edward M. Bergin, ARM2c, reports his first royal flush since hitting the Sopac area, which may have helped him send an allotment back to the Hospital Trust in Providence toward finishing his college work at Brown after the war.

1945

Pvt. Vincent Galli who was here at Brown with the Pre-meteorology C Unit has now gone to Canada for further training in the Air Corps.

Conrad Brown returned recently from more than a year with the American Field Service, wearing a Polish Eagle, an African Star, and the crusader's shield insigne of the British Eighth Army. Now he's in the American Army and hopes to get into the ski troops.

Pvt. Thomas J. Luby, Jr., writes from Camp Carson that he is one of 10 Brown men that he knows of with his Infantry division. We've asked him to tell us who the others are.

Kenneth Lindsay, Jr., USAAF, was at the Single Engine Advanced School at

▶ ▶ Pembroke Chronicle

BY GERTRUDE ALLEN MacCONNELL

Alumnae Day

▶ ▶ MORE than 500 alumnae attended the 1944 Alumnae Day on June 17. The return of this unusually large group, in spite of wartime difficulties, was a tribute to Dr. Mary E. Woolley '94, who was a special guest of the College and of the Alumnae Association on the occasion of her 50th reunion.

The day's program began with the luncheons planned by the classes observing official reunions, as well as the score or more of other classes who have an annual luncheon on Alumnae Day. The majority of luncheons were held at hotels and clubs, some at the homes of members, and one at the Pembroke Field House.

The luncheons were followed by the business meeting of the Alumnae Association, held at two o'clock in the auditorium of Alumnae Hall, at which Ruth Peterson Watjen '19' president of the Association, presided. After the meeting Dean Morriss spoke to the alumnae on "The College in Wartime." Dr. Woolley then addressed the group on the subject: "The College Woman After Wartime."

Following the speeches a reception for Dr. Woolley was held in the Crystal Room. On this occasion the long line of alumnae and friends who came to greet Dr. Woolley was an expression of their sincere admiration and affection for their distinguished fellow alumna. In the line also were the members of the Class of 1894 from "over on the hill" who brought their warm greetings. Dr. Woolley was assisted in receiving by Dean Morriss, Mrs. Watien, and the Alumnae Day Chairman, Ethel Humphrey Anderson '29. Ices and cakes were served by Carr.

The 1944 Alumnae Day seemed to have something of the atmosphere of a "homecoming day." Dr. Woolley's presence and the fact that the alumnae serving at the reception were the mothers of undergraduates or of other alumnae emphasized the "family" feeling.

The Reunion. Committee consisted of Ethel Humphrey Anderson '29' Chairman; Helen Daniels Andrews '15' Vice Chairman; Mary B. Leonard '99' Lottie Devlin Ward '04' Irma Gyllenberg Cull and M. Grace Frost '09' Elena Lovell Maymon '14' Edith Goff Miner '19' Dorothy C. Maguire '24' D. Audrey Reed '29' Mary T. Mc-

Moore Field, Mission, Tex. in May when we heard from his father. His home address: 310—19th St., S. E., Cedar Rapids, Ia.

A/S Richard S. Blacher wrote recently from the Naval Hospital at Sampson to subscribe for the magazine. "Although I keep in contact with Brown men — a few are stationed here—like all of us I devour any Brunoniana I can lay my hands on and thus I read my copy from cover to cover." Dick likes the work and set-up at Sampson but adds, "I guess we'd wish we were back on the hill wherever we were."

Cpl. Robert W. Noyes was up in Kodiak Island, Alaska, with an aircraft warning company when he wrote Joe Cook '43' Said he liked it, too.

Carthy and Dorothy Greene Vernet '34' Barbara Gilbert, Elizabeth Goodale and Edna Murphy '39' Grace Hundt Viall '41' Hope B. Brown '43' and Ruth Cunningham '44'

The beautiful flowers, which added so much to the festive appearance of Alumnae Hall, were arranged by Nettie Butler Rice '09 and Marguerite Reid Wetmore '02 as chairmen, assisted by Beulah Sheldon Bellows '07, Agnes Johnson Wrinn '18, Elisabeth Rice Smart '37, and Lucille Bowers Keegan '39. Ices were served under the chairmanship of Irma Gyllenberg Cull '09 and Mildred Cutler Kinne '14 was in charge of ushers for the reception. ◀

The Garden Restaurant

THIS DELIGHTFUL ROOM, host to hundreds of
visitors to Rhode Island each week, features
the music of a well-known dance orchestra
and incidental entertainment. You'll enjoy
dinner or supper here, especially when you
have guests to entertain. There is no 20% tax
at dinner up to 9 p. m.

PROVIDENCE-BILTMORE

CPSIA information can be obtained
at www.ICGtesting.com
Printed in the USA
BVHW04*1054170918
527708BV00015B/2224/P

9 780484 344692